Praise for Ro

"This author is worthy of yo
entertaining and informed writer."
Graham Lawler. www.graham-lawler.com

"The author's professional approach strikes again."
A.J. Portugal. On *Island Interludes*.

"This book catalogues Rosalie's Italy experience with
food, religion, stunning attractions, transport, and the
epic history that this country has to offer . . . through
culturally and historically rich places including Rome,
Florence, Venice, Sorrento, and wider Italy. An
outstanding book for anyone that enjoys travel."
Jamie Cawley. Australia. Amazon. *The Long Leg of
Italy*.

"A gifted author who can bring her travel books alive.
She has a wonderful sense of the ridiculous and her style
as a raconteur means that the reader feels she is talking
personally." Judith Sharman on *Just Us Two*.

"Another great book by Rosalie Marsh that should not
be missed. The flow of words employed to narrate it, is
in itself most refreshing." Joseph Abela, Author, on
Chasing Rainbows.

"A wonderful story that takes the reader to the heart of
the place that Rosalie Marsh loves so much.
Jean Mead, Author, on *ORANGES*.

"A thoroughly enjoyable and well-observed read."
Alan Bissell on *The Long Leg of Italy*.

Also by Rosalie Marsh

Just Us Two Travel Series
Just Us Two: Ned and Rosie's Gold Wing Discovery.
Chasing Rainbows: with Just Us Two.
The Long Leg of Italy: Explore with Just Us Two.

Fiction
ORANGES: A Journey.

Lifelong Learning: Personal Effectiveness Guides
Lifelong Learning: A View from the Coalface.
Release Your Potential: Making Sense of Personal and Professional Development.
Skills for Employability Part One: Pre-Employment.
Skills for Employability Part Two: Moving into Employment.
Talking the Talk: Getting the Message Across.

About the Author

Rosalie Marsh writes on a variety of topics from hilarious biographical travel adventures to more serious stuff based on personal development – which are light-hearted and user-friendly.

Marsh says: "In the midst of pots and pans I often dreamed of writing as many story lines popped up in my head. My wide range of activities provided me with a rich seam of material."

As 'born-again' bikers on a Honda Gold Wing motorbike, Marsh and her husband found their lost youth travelling on their own –Just Us Two – in Europe,

Later, this award-winning story developed into the 'Just Us Two' series of biographical travel adventures.

Retiring to concentrate on her writing, Marsh drew on her skills and experiences in travel and adult education. From this, the series of Lifelong Learning Personal Effectiveness Guides developed – each a big workshop in a small package.

Embracing digital solutions, all books are always available worldwide in print and e-book formats for most devices.

Rosalie Marsh writes under a pen name.

Connect with Rosalie at:

http://www.discover-rosalie.com

http://www.discover-rosalie.blogspot.com

Twitter: @Rosalie Marsh, @JustUsTwoTravel, @LifelongD

www.facebook.com/rosalie.marsh.JustUsTwoTravel?ref=hl

Island
Interludes

Rosalie Marsh

Christal Publishing

CHRISTAL PUBLISHING
christalpublishing.com

First published 2017 by Christal Publishing.
ISBN 978-1-908302-43-4. Perfect Bound Soft Cover.
ISBN 978-1-908302 52-6. Hardback.
ISBN 978-1-908302-45-8. eBook – ePub.
ISBN 978-1-908302-47-2. eBook – ePub (Smashwords Edition).

British Library Cataloguing in Publication Data.
A catalogue record for this book is available from the British Library.
This book is printed on acid-free paper from responsible sources.

Facts have been verified by the videos taken at the time, personal notes, reference to the Internet, and maps. Some reference has been made to The Long Leg of Italy by kind permission of the author.

Map of the North Atlantic by anniebissett.com (national geographic expeditions.com) by kind permission.
Maps of the Mediterranean Sea, Sao Miguel Island, and Canary Islands courtesy of commons.wikimedia.org.
Postcard map of Gran Canaria ©A.Murillo
Wikipedia references/links/maps courtesy of
https://creativecommons.org/licenses/by/2.0/uk/

WREXHAM. WALES. UK

Acknowledgements

My thanks go to my Maltese friends — Joseph Abela, Author, who comes from Marsa (Maltese: Il-Marsa). Marsa is twinned with Bridgewater in the UK where Joseph now lives; Marthese Morris, my friend and ex-colleague, who was born and lived in Qormi before her marriage was also generous of her time; their support in reading and clarification of the chapter on the brave and valiant island of Malta was invaluable.

Thank you to our long-time friends Joan and Rob who first introduced us to the diversity and beauty of the sunny island of Tenerife in the Islas Canarias (Canary Islands). Our exploration then of many parts of the island formed the basis of more visits over the years when we also enjoyed the company of friends Bob and Terri whose visits to Tenerife usually coincided with ours. They introduced us to the Masca Valley in the north-western tip of Tenerife.

Finally, my husband Allen who has been invaluable in correcting and refining the more technical, cultural and factual aspects of my writings without taking away my own more romantic view.

Images

Meandering the Mediterranean.

1. Map. Mediterranean Sea.
2. Photo. View of the coast from Castel Mola. Sicily.
3. Photo. View of Giardini Naxos from Taormina. Sicily.
4. Photo. View from Castel Mola over the rooftops. Sicily.
5. Photo. A red London bus in Syracuse. Sicily.
6. Photo. Portomaso Marina. St. Julian's Bay. Malta.
7. Photo. Valletta. Malta.
8. Photo. A church in Valletta. Malta.
9. Photo. Lace-making in Lefkara. Cyprus.

Images

Atlantic Adventure.

10. Map. Islands of the North Atlantic.
11. Map. The island of São Miguel in the Azores.
12. Photo. A man on a donkey. São Miguel.
13. Photo. Ponta Delgada at Christmas. São Miguel.
14. Photo. Church with 100 steps. São Miguel.
15. Photo. Sete Cidades. Green and blue lake. São Miguel.
16. Photo. Lago de Fogo – Fire Lake. São Miguel.
17. Photo. A lake in the Furnas Valley. São Miguel.
18. Photo. Monte – riding down in a basket to Funchal. Madeira.
19. Map. Canary Islands.
20. Photo. Camels in Timanfaya National Park. Lanzarote.
21. Photo. Needles of rock. Los Hervideros. Lanzarote.
22. Photo. Camels on the beach. Fuerteventura.
23. Photo. Boom Trike Adventure. Fuerteventura.
24. Map. Pictorial postcard photo. Gran Canaria.
25. Photo. Arucas Rum Distillery. Gran Canaria.
26. Photo. Puerto De Mogan. Gran Canaria.
27. Photo. Plaque of the Convento de Hermigua. La Gomera.
28. Photo. Sand Painting at La Casa de los Balcones. La Orotava. Tenerife.
29. Photo. Helicopter Ride. Tenerife
30. Photo. El Drago-Dragon Tree. Icod de los Vinos. Tenerife.

Contents

Meandering in the Mediterranean.

Sicily.
Malta.
Cyprus.

Atlantic Adventure.

Azores.
Madeira.
Lanzarote.
Fuerteventura.
Gran Canaria.
La Gomera.
Tenerife.
Reflections: A Return to Tenerife.

Bibliography.
Further Reading.

Meandering
in the
Mediterranean

Sicily

An island of mystery, sunshine, and untold stories. An island dominated by a volcano that erupts when it is angry and the molten lava needs release into the sky as it forces its way from the bowels of the mountain. An island that stretches back into the mists of time, drawing you into its deep mysterious soul as it hugs its secrets of the past to itself. An island at the foot of Italy that floats in the Mediterranean Sea with the warm waters of the Tyrrhenian and Ionian Seas lapping at its northern and eastern shores.

In *the Long Leg of Italy*, we left our story as we arrived in Messina in Sicily on the ferry from Reggio de Calabria in southern Italy. As the coach rolled down the ramp, we couldn't help reflecting on our first visit in 2005 when we had taken the train to Messina to check out the logistics of coming across on our Honda Gold Wing converted trike. The story continues. . . .

******

The romance and mystery of Sicily had always made a pull on my imagination. As we had had our wings clipped so to speak in 2004, the big question was, 'Where do we go next?'

I had pored over the holiday brochures many times but in some way, was held back – it was a long way into the unknown. However, we reasoned that if we were with a travel company, we would be safe. Looking at the maps and remembering earlier stories, I thought that the island would be uninhabited. Mount Etna did seem close to the towns and it was still active. Bearing all this in mind and looking at the included trips of the holiday, I persuaded Allen – using the history and archaeology as a 'carrot' – and off we flew in November 2005 to Catania for Giardini Naxos by the sea.

Two days before [Sunday], on waking, I stretched my muscles languorously to the full length of my body whereupon my back seized up. With a howl of pain, I found that the slightest movement was impossible. Allen came back from church with instructions from friends.

'Tell her that she has to get on that plane even if she has to crawl.'

By now, after taking pain relief tablets, the pain was lessening and we set off to see my mother who was celebrating her birthday. After I had assured her – much to her astonishment – that I most certainly *would* be going on holiday and not cancelling it she promptly gave me my late father's sturdy walking stick to use whilst we were away.

The seaside town of Giardini Naxos spreads along a wide, sandy, curved bay on the eastern side of the island, some distance from the ancient town of Taormina in the hills. The village of Castel Mola sitting above it on the mountain stands guard as it looks out to sea. Being on the promenade, the hotel overlooked the bay with direct access to the promenade. The small secluded terrace at the front of the hotel was a pleasant place to relax. There were potted plants of all sizes and shapes to add to the air of tranquillity while you looked out across the bay towards Taormina.

We were lucky enough to have a huge room that was a suite with a separate seating area furnished with two settees. There was also a furnished balcony overlooking the promenade and the sea with excellent views along the whole of the bay. From there was a clear view across the bay to the 'must see' town and village of Taormina and Castel Mola in the hills above. We looked forward to the options of many days' personal exploration, not only into Giardini Naxos old town itself at the other end of the bay, but into the hills high above the bay. With our first day drawing to a close, I was entranced to see the lights from Castel Mola twinkling in the darkness as they shone out from secret nooks and crannies like stars, down past Taormina to the bay below. I came to love this quiet time each evening as I rested on the balcony in the balmy night air to watch these lights shining across the bay and dream of times gone by.

The morning after our arrival, as usual, I was up early to watch from our balcony the boats bobbing in the harbour as the sun rose at seven o'clock. I was both startled and entranced to hear the church bells ringing out to the tune of 'Ave Maria'. Making a quick grab for the camcorder, I hastened to record this beautiful sound breaking the quiet of the early morning sunrise. Through the viewfinder as I panned and zoomed across the wide, sweeping bay, I could clearly see Taormina and Castel Mola nestling into the hillside. Before breakfast on that first morning, there were a lot of policemen swarming around in front of the hotel.

'What can be up?' we wondered as I pointed this out to Allen. We later learned that there was a conference on in the hotel.

******

As usual the [Saga 50+] holiday started with a Welcome Meeting the morning after our arrival. This took place in another part of an adjoining hotel. These are not obligatory but useful to attend as the Rep. shares much information about the locality, the trips on offer, facilities of the hotel, arrangements for meals, and anything else which they feel is useful. The included excursions on this holiday at that time were to Mount Etna and Syracuse – both full day trips. We opted to go on these, there is always a choice even if included, but conscious of limitations we decided against others to the south of the island such as Agrigento and Piazza Armenia. Our information was that these last two would involve much walking on uneven ground; we opted to do some exploring of our own instead and wander at will.

******

After the Welcome Meeting, our Rep. took us on the usual orienteering walk to point out some significant points of interest. As I was still walking slowly with my walking stick, I decided to rest on the promenade wall while the rest of the group had their fill of history and local folklore as I could not keep up. I was happy to sit quietly and dream while the sea air and sunshine assaulted my senses.

In the distance, from my perch on the sea wall, I watched Allen forge his way to the front of the group in order not to miss any vital information. The eager group became smaller and smaller as they faded into the distance, heading towards the archaeological remains at the far end of the town where the bay jutted out into the sea. As usual, the Rep. was very informative.

We usually enjoy these orienteering walks, as they give you a flavour of the main points of interest, chemist shops, post office, cafés, etc., so that you are not left floundering.

On this occasion, I was happy to absorb the sights and sounds around me as I gazed out to sea and took in the tranquillity.

Castel Mola and Taormina.

Being November, night falls quite early and, as I have said earlier, the lights on the hillside are very pretty. The castle at Castel Mola high above the sea, is lit up and shines like a beacon in the darkness. It seems to draw you in with a promise of long gone secrets to be told – if only you will make the journey.

You can reach Castel Mola in a variety of ways.

Option Number One – walk up the whole way – **not** an option.

Option Number Two – catch a bus to Taormina and Castel Mola but as the bus stops in the square at Castel Mola, there is then a climb of about fifty-six steps.

Option Number Three was the most favourable – take a taxi up to the top and walk back down to the square and wait for the bus to take us back down to Giardini Naxos.

Decision made, a taxi-ride it was as a climb of about fifty-six steps was out of the question. Climbing higher and higher above the sea the taxi driver tooted his horn on the switchback road and tight bends to warn oncoming traffic of our presence. As we wended our way to our destination the panoramic view over the bay far below revealed rocky outcrops spread out into the sea.

The weather was good; the sun shone in the November sky casting its light onto the sparkling sea below. Everywhere, flowering shrubs splashed a patchwork of colour in the verdant countryside.

Alighting from the taxi, the mist shrouded everything so high in the clouds was this village hanging off the mountainside. Castel Mola is a very ancient village full of attractive and charming stone buildings.

The stupendous and breath-taking views were well worth the journey. Leaning over a wall, we could see how the road zig-zagged back to the coast down the sheer drop through the hillside where red-roofed houses were dotted about among the lush vegetation.

VIEW FROM CASTEL MOLA ABOVE TAORMINA.

'The paths marked in red go down to Taormina. That's quite good actually,'

I can be heard to comment on the film.

Wandering through the town, dark-eyed locals silently watched us as they scurried about their daily tasks or stood in groups in the mist. Women chatted and gossiped as they went about their daily tasks, meeting up for that daily tit-bit of news and gossip which was food of life to them in their isolated village. The few shops displayed their wares outside even though, being November, it was the end of their main season – for tourists that is, locals still had to live – but the winter warmth also drew tourists at all times of the year.

Samples of cutwork embroidery in their embroidery hoops took me back to my childhood sewing lessons, whilst they vied for attention with all manner of fruits, wine, and everyday objects.

We walked slowly, puffing and panting, to the ruins of the ancient Castel [Castle] and, oh! What a view. Using the camcorder viewfinder, I zoomed down the mountain across to our hotel and the archaeological site at the far end of the bay in Giardini Naxos. The coastline was amazing – it was like looking at a map. Although almost in the clouds, the curve of the bay and coastline to Catania, which swept out like fingers or an open jaw before curving back, was laid out before our eyes.

The ruined castle high above the village was a testament to life in ancient times. The steps through the ruins needed care so as not to slip as the steps were damp in the mist.

Back in the square, we sat on a bench for a rest, whereupon a man got into conversation, asking us how we had made the journey up to the village. He tried to offer us a cheaper ride down. This we resisted as we had decided to find a bus to take us back down the steep and winding hill.

The square in Castel Mola, laid underfoot with a lovely pattern of grey and white stonework, was busy with cars and vans parked at will; it was mainly surrounded by large, substantial houses built of grey stone with long square windows and doors. Built into the sheer rock of the mountain they were largely protected from the elements. It was a bit chilly in the damp air as we waited but eventually a bus trundled up to the square.

The bus ride down to Taormina from Castel Mola was quite hairy. Oh, how we ached to be on the Gold Wing motorbike. What an exhilarating challenge that would be. Ever adventurous and optimistic of our abilities, we discussed the possibility – seriously – of riding through Italy to Calabria in the toe of Italy and crossing into Sicily. Could we? Should we? Yes, and without more ado decided to make a trip while we were here to the port at Messina to reccae the lie of the land and the logistics of our proposal. (Another dream on hold.)

VIEW FROM CASTEL MOLA OVER THE ROOFTOPS.

However, as we arrived now in Taormina we were delighted to see orange trees full of fruit.

'We are now in the shopping centre,' I am heard to comment on the video, 'We will see what I can spend.'

'Or not,' came a firm rejoinder.

The smart shops and businesses vied for attention beside old buildings and ruins of ancient times. There was a lovely ice-cream parlour which we simply had to sample. Timeless Taormina, perched on the hillside above the sea engraved itself on my heart.

The Greeks and Romans would have had warning of any invaders heading towards the island, enabling them to prepare for defence and keep their inhabitants in safety. Narrow streets tumbled downwards between ancient buildings via steep steps where glimpses of the sea appeared at every twist and turn.

The narrowness of the streets was not a concern to the many car drivers who simply waited their turn in the heavy traffic of cars and noisy scooters or indeed, to those who simply parked up at will. We stopped in the beautiful wide square to look at the view down to the coast and what a view as the hillside stretched down past flowering shrubs and palm trees to the sea. It struck us, as we gazed at the preserved buildings, that on the continent everyone is proud of their heritage and, rather than seeking to destroy and cover up, fly the flag and proclaim their roots and history.

Looking up towards the tops of buildings whose balconies overflowed with colourful plants, through the huddle of satellite dishes hung from the tops of the walls and very high television aerials sprouted from the rooftops, a glimpse of Castel Mola, where it sat proudly high above all else as it guarded its inhabitants from invaders in ancient times, peeped out.

In contrast, the wide squares reflected current daily life as outdoor cafes and restaurants abounded in the shade of umbrellas and leafy trees.

One day, we caught the bus into Taormina. Our plan was to explore the ruins of the Greek Theatre. Alighting from the bus at the bus station – that was a small tarmaced area off the main road where buildings jostled for space at either side – we eventually wended our way into the town among the profusion of cars and vans parked in every available space. I say eventually as I kept stopping to film the views, sights and sounds while Allen waited patiently, waving to me to indicate that he was moving on regardless.

Reaching the town, it was easy to see how it was built on the mountainside, such was the sheer drop. Taormina is blessed with a glorious jumbled profusion of elegant shops, ancient churches and buildings, many restaurants, narrow streets where you can see glimpses of the sea in the distance, and a huge, wide piazza perched on the edge of the mountain.

Strolling along the wide, tree-lined road leading to the Greek Theatre, we were enchanted to see in one of the many shops a window full of stick-like figures made from strips of metal, nuts and bolts. They were made up into figures working at different occupations. I was fascinated by the lady working at a typewriter, a man on a motorcycle, a figure wielding a hammer. There were quite a few of motorcyclists, some on bikes with extremely extended forks. We had our eye on one but decided against taking the plunge. The list of occupations was endless.

Suddenly, the sun took *off* its hat and the rain came down; we were amused to see the stallholders putting away sun hats and quickly wheel out one of umbrellas. Needless to say, they did a roaring trade as we purchased our umbrella of choice.

Wandering through the arches into the vast expanse of the curved Greek Theatre we unexpectedly found that there was an abundance of orange trees growing and flowering in the sunshine which ripened the oranges nestling among the deep green leaves. From the Greek Theatre, the eye follows a line down a clear view to Giardini Naxos sitting in the curve of the bay far below. Sheltering under our umbrella, we explored at will. The narrow, low tunnels in the ruins led to small rooms and passages where stone benches were engraved in Greek lettering. What was amazing also was to find words scratched into some of the bricks. Were these the names of the bricklayers who toiled in the Sicilian heat? Or were they simply the names of the streets or area in which we stood?

Eventually coming out into the amphitheatre, we could see tall, white columns flanking the high, imposing arches which had stood for centuries. They were awesome when, on reflection, you realized just how long they had been there undisturbed apart from erosion of time. Allen eschewed the umbrella, not caring if he got a little wet as he took a multitude of photographs. I meanwhile, was busy filming the wide curved seating area, trying to imagine how it would have been when full of people cheering, laughing, and shouting while watching productions. Don't forget that the Greeks were there before the Romans so you can soon work out how old it was.

Allen was fascinated by a loose brick in the walls of the archway to the theatre which was built many years BC. The bricks were red, long, and thin and he [Allen] had a high old time examining and exploring all facets of the brick which he patiently and enthusiastically explained to me He placed his fingers in the finger imprints of that long ago Greek bricklayer and was awed. The brick had finger prints in it where the bricklayer – no doubt in dress/costume of the time of a short tunic – had picked it up before it was *quite* dry.

'Are you sure that you weren't here two thousand years ago, making bricks?' I cheekily queried.

'They weren't quite dry.' Laughingly, he carefully placed the brick back into the wall of the arch.

The mortar in-between the bricks was thick and stony. Possibly mixed with lava? Surprisingly, the mortar did not come to the edge of the bricks as ours do in buildings. Perhaps that was design or erosion of time. In the midst of all this were tall palm trees which waved in the clear mountain air as Allen continued his examination of this wonderful preserved ruin.

By now the soft, gentle rain had stopped as quickly as it had started and we were able to appreciate even more the sense of timelessness as we gazed around the curve of this great amphitheatre slumbering in the sunshine. Heading out of the theatre, we stopped again at the shop which sold the wonderful metal creations of all kinds of occupations.

'What are they made of? Just bits of metal?'

One figure, quite a large one, was made from a mixture of copper and a grey metal. For pantaloons, they had used an upturned cone shape.

'Aren't they good?' I was astonished.

'Do you want one?'

'Want one? What?'

'The man on a trike,' came firmly in my shell-like ear.

Of course, the 'one' in question was of a man on a boom trike with its long front forks. I ought to have known.

Taking a bus down through the winding roads to Giardini Naxos was another experience. At every twist and turn we were afforded a different, unforgettable view, A different glimpse at every twist and turn of red-roofed buildings below us – the roofs of buildings below us became a common sight as we toiled up and down the mountainside during our visit. Creamy stone walls and gateposts held secure tall, intricate, wrought iron gates which heralded the entrance to a property, while the roads were lined with palm trees of all kinds. They were also lined with parked cars on the bends and how the bus driver missed them is a testament to his skill and experience – and the lock on the steering wheel. Some of the houses were painted a warm apricot/orange colour which formed a colourful contrast to the dark green of the abundant trees.

Far down below, we could see rocky outcrops spreading out into the sea. We were not to know then that we would be fortunate enough in a few years to spend a few days in this delightful spot which we came to know as Mazzaro. More of that later.

I must say that Allen, not being a good traveller, concentrated on arriving in one piece as he mastered the shaky journey. Alighting in Giardini Naxos we made our way back to our hotel by the sea for a quiet drink on its sea front terrace

That evening we were treated to the delightful and lively sound of a group of musicians playing an accordion, guitar and a whistle-type of instrument. Not confining themselves to local folk music, they also played some of the favourite tunes of the British contingent.

Mount Etna.

'It is seven o'clock, the sun is rising and it is set to be another beautiful day.'

Once again, I was absorbing the sights and sounds of a sleepy town from our balcony as it woke to the day.

Many boats bobbed in the sea while others were pulled up onto the sands where they rested in the shelter of the bay as no doubt, they had done for centuries.

Our day long trip to Mount Etna took us through a delightful town of Zafferana built on the slopes of the mountain; at around five hundred metres we were about half-way up to Mount Etna. Wikipedia tells us that,

"Zafferana Etnea (Sicilian Zafarana) is a commune in the Province of Catania in the Italian region Sicily, located about 160 kilometres southeast of Palermo and about 20 kilometres north of Catania."

Stopping for coffee we had the opportunity to explore a little of this mountain town with its elegant, mainly square, buildings. Zafarana has a beautiful cream coloured stone, twin-towered church. Many steps lead up from the small piazza to the church entrance. We spent time exploring the main body of the church and the many side chapels.

Outside, many men were sitting around leading us to think that unemployment must be high; tourist coaches vied for space as they disgorged their passengers into the square. The wide, elegant streets, bordered with parked cars, were lined with trees on the other side of the road. The small park was enhanced in the middle by the most beautiful fountain with many jets of water spilling high into the sky before falling in a noisy rush and splutter of spray to the huge, circular bowl below. From the spectacular, lava-stone balcony the views over the eastern slopes were incredible.

'Smile,' I entreated Allen whom today, was wearing his favourite black polo shirt with the North Wales Wings logo. Strolling through the square and down the busy street, we admired the red cauliflowers set out in front of the fruit and vegetable shop. Yes, red.

'Cauliflowers?'

'Yes,' came the reply.

'Well. why are they pink, erm, purple?'

'It must be what is in the soil,' replied my fount of all knowledge. (Yes, he really does know a lot about a lot of things.)

Inside the shop, viewed through the full-length windows, were glimpses of other products on display. With no more time left to linger, we re-joined the coach.

Continuing on our way, our guide stopped the coach to allow us to have a look at the 1884 lava flow. What an experience to be able to walk on solidified lava. The more agile people with sturdier shoes, wandered further afield as they trod around huge boulders on the solidified lava. The guide told us that it travelled seven miles dropping by twenty degrees Celsius from one thousand to nine hundred and eighty degrees Celsius. In one instance, the lava had just missed a village by some miracle.

Allen explained that sometimes the lava folds in on itself, doesn't cool and goes down a tunnel underneath.

We were allowed to stop to have a look and take photos and of course, try the local cakes, honey and chocolate drink which were being sold by the roadside by the ever-resourceful local villagers.

Arriving at Mount Etna, we left the coach and went in the cable car which rattled its way further up the mountain to two thousand five hundred metres. Panning around to the black lava, I recorded, while catching my breath in the thin mountain air that,

'We are now on Mount. Etna. We are at a height of two thousand five hundred metres. Hiding behind the clouds is, I think, the crater at the top.'

Panning around further, the cable car went higher.

'There are the jeeps which will takes those who want to venture up there to the crater at three thousand metres. [Nine thousand feet.] And there is the cable car station from where we have just come up the mountain.'

The film shows clearly how that last set of posts and pulleys, on the edge of the mountain, is on a flat area before it goes into the station. It also shows the cable car being swallowed by the clouds as it goes on its descent back down the mountain. Allen was very brave in only having a pullover for warmth and not a jacket. He also was keeper of the packed lunch prepared by the hotel staff.

The landscape covered with black lava as far as they eye could see was surreal. It was like a forbidden planet of times gone by. We decided not to go in the jeep to the crater but opted to have a warm drink in the café and a wander around in this desolate and black mountain.

'The cable car used to go to the summit but after it was destroyed it was not built as high. It stops here.'

Allen continued to inform me. What would I do without him? How did he know that?

One of the party commented that his film would simply be of black rock. We laughed and said that my thing was to photograph feet when I had forgotten to switch off the camcorder.

'Oh, feet? We have thousands of feet.'

The clouds now came down and, as the cable car station was closing the rangers urged everyone to board quickly and get down the mountain back to safety.

'We are on the cable car on the way down because they have closed the cable car. The clouds are too low and there are a few specks glass on the wet.'

'Glass on the wet?

'I mean wet on the glass.' I quickly corrected myself as Allen laughed.

He continued to say – quite inconsequently – that the digestive drink we had been given the previous had quite spoiled his dinner.

'They give it free, do they?' he continued.

'That was a taster.' I assured him.

'Dear me, if you had bought a bottle of that without tasting . . .,' he trailed off not bearing to think of the consequences. (He doesn't drink alcohol as it doesn't suit him.)

'Fancy giving that as a present to somebody,' I went on as I continued to film the rocks on the way down.

As we rattled and banged our way down visibility became clearer. We could see rocks below and the chair lifts which are used in the skiing season making their way up to the cable car station. Suddenly, the cable car stopped and we hung mid-air. We all looked at each other in consternation,

'We are going to swing in mid-air all night, are we?' I wondered aloud.

There were all sorts of dry comments being bandied around; more to calm some of the nervous passengers in the cable car. Some of our fellow passengers were quite perturbed. All we could see now down the mountain were the occasional poles and wires holding the mechanism and wispy clouds obscuring our view. It was so quiet, still and eerie with no means of communication.

All at once we started to move again which meant that we had a good view of the mechanism as the car slowly glided down the mountainside. Then, there was a very unnerving and noisy creaking and banging in the enveloping mist as we rocked from side-to-side with the ski chairs silently, eerily, passing us at our side.

Crashing down the mountain is not something you want to consider at the best of times and certainly not down an active volcanic mountain prone to erupting. With more violent creaking, banging and rocking we slowly edged down the mountainside which now looked a little clearer. It was certainly greener. With the mist dispersing we could see rows of ski-lifts on the other side to us.

'Is that all they sit in when they are going skiing?' My amazement knew no bounds.

'I am trying to figure out how it works. They lift the bar up, sit in and the bar comes down over your head,' surmised Allen.

It was quite a picture to see all the ski lifts working their way along the cables, like soldiers in formation, as they ascended the mountain which now was covered in yellow patches of vegetation.

'We have stopped again. We haven't far to go.'

I commented before we set off again to reach safety – much to the profound relief of other occupants in the cable car. Well, at least Etna did not erupt while we were up there.

To Messina.

I said earlier that we had decided to go to Messina to look at the logistics of coming across on the Gold Wing trike and where the ferries came in etc. We had already been to the Railway Station in Giardini Naxos to find out times of trains and one fine morning we set off for another adventurous day of exploration.

The Giardini Naxos railway station is a truly remarkable edifice and a relic of days gone by. A detailed description is called for as I simply must share with you the elegance and colour of the design.

In the entrance, the ceiling is made up of intricately decorated panels painted in brilliant gold, bronzes, reds and blues with chandeliers hanging down. Yes. Chandeliers in a railway station. They were huge with an intricately designed ring of metal suspended from the ceiling. On this ring, lamps were fixed around the edge. High arched doors lead to the corridors from where the waiting rooms for passengers were tucked away. The train platforms were reached from this corridor. Tall, ornate columns supported these covered platforms; grey and white tiled floors created a pleasant ambience and unhurried atmosphere in this glimpse into times gone by.

Outside, high on the walls was an example of the very modern technology of the arrivals and departure screens. One proclaimed 'Partenze' [Departures]. The modern twenty-first century trains and technology were a stark contrast to this ornate and well-preserved station. – an important part of Sicily's past.

On the platform, a white and green modern train was about to leave. The guard, wearing a red pillbox style hat, waited for the announcements to finish before making sure that everyone was on the train safely and all the doors locked. With a blow on his whistle and a wave of his paddle [flags seem to be obsolete now], he signalled to the driver who gently moved the train out of the station, picking up speed as he went.

Across the other side of the track we could clearly see the blue station sign proclaiming 'Taormina – Giardini'.

The journey took us along the very scenic but rocky coast. The railway line literally hugs the shore with the main road vying for space as it follows the perimeter of the island. Over the fifty-minute or so journey, we left many towns and villages far behind as signs for Taormina, Letojanni, Roccalumera, Ali Terme, to name a few, flashed by. All, sat above the rocky coast where the Ionian Sea ebbed and flowed as it lazily crashed away against the rocks far below. The same sea that all those years ago, the Greeks and Romans would have looked down upon.

In Messina, our first task on leaving the railway station was to walk to the nearby port to look at the ferry and other boats to see how it all worked. The warmer weather suited Allen and we comfortably watched as a variety of boats plied back and forth between Messina and Reggio de Calabria on the mainland.

'Is that a hydrofoil there?'

'I think that is,' replied he who knows.

There was a high-speed one which easily disgorged its passengers – more like a bus really. We watched with interest as the workings of the port carried on regardless of what was going on around it.

Our quest was to look at the boats which took vehicles and watched with great interest as one came in to moor up. The vehicles waiting to board left a passageway for the ones disembarking.

'It is not unlike Holyhead [Anglesey, Wales] really, is it?' I am heard to comment. Apart from boarding arrangements that is.

Meanwhile, sitting on the harbour wall at the side of the ferry ramp with his feet dangling over the water, a local fisherman unconcernedly carried on with his fishing, watching for the fish to bite the bait at the end of his fishing line, while passengers disembarked as wagons and cars rolled down the ramp. It all seemed very laid back yet efficient as the parking of vehicles was allowed right up to the harbour wall on the quayside. There were no massive ramps or officialdom in evidence. Simply – on and off. Just like a bus terminal.

Intriguingly, there were train lines running along the quayside where the ferry train runs along before being loaded onto a special kind of boat for the trip to the mainland. This truly astounded me. To think that you could stop on the train while you crossed the water.

Watching a crowd of embarking foot passengers heading towards the lowering ramp [bow of the ship] I was enthralled.

'It looks like those foot passengers are just going to walk on.'

'Yes, and some are walking off and there are some waiting to get on this one here,' Allen patiently explained.

'In England, you have a separate gangway for foot passengers.'

'Yes. Well that's why I wanted to see where this fellow pulled up.' A motorbiker was waiting to embark and had parked by the railings.

Watching in fascinated awe, a long, articulated lorry got stuck on the ramp as the underneath scraped the bottom of the ramp. Willing hands and voices joined in the *mêlée* to give directions. Here a bit, left a bit, forward. It was all very nerve-racking for everyone but eventually the wagon came free and it edged its way down to the safe ground of the harbour side.

'They earn their money, don't they?' I was truly impressed even though holding my breath in wonder.

Meanwhile all the cars, wagons, scooters, and pedestrians in the queue waited patiently before they could embark. A girl on a scooter waited only inches away to go up the ram as soon as the wagon was clear.

Bear in mind that in the midst of this chaotic scene, the lone fisherman with his simple rod and bait, carried on nonchalantly with his task of trying to catch his dinner.

'How can they allow that?' I queried. 'To have someone fishing?'

'I don't know.'

There was no segregation of vehicle types. They all took their chance in a mixed queue while foot passengers strolled amongst them to board the ferry. What a refreshing free for all.

With the wagon edging off, wagons, cars, motorbikes, scooters, and foot passengers waiting to embark and a fisherman fishing between the sea wall and ships, it was all quite an entertainment to say the least.

Satisfied with our logistics and that bringing the bike across really *was* a possibility, it was time to find a restaurant for lunch. Strolling away from the port towards the town, trams with two coaches concertinaed together rolled quietly down the streets, vying for attention with cars, bicycles, and pedestrians. No one would argue with these very modern beasts of transport, giving way easily as they rolled by. Dodging these very modern trams which glided around the corner of the street, we crossed a tree-lined square in the city centre.

The stone seats in the huge square that was lined with an avenue of leafy trees, were mainly occupied by young people – some of whom were carrying placards – who appeared to be gathering for a student rally. Waiting to cross a side road over to a restaurant that we had noticed, a lady stopped by me and with signals, admonished me to 'put away the camcorder. Hide it.'

She appeared concerned that someone could snatch it off me and was worried at what she deemed my stupidity. Hurriedly, I did as she indicated, hiding the camcorder in my capacious bag. We did not want to linger in Messina due to the apparent student rally gathering and did not want to get caught up in anything. But first, food.

With camcorder safely stored away, we crossed the road. The restaurant that we had seen had a 'secure' entrance. It was also above a bank – a tall grey building. Security was tight. We thought this quite unusual but I expect that land was at a premium. In our other travels, we had noticed that buildings in towns and cities were often multi-use.

The secure entrance was, in fact, a marvellous piece of engineering. If you wanted the bank downstairs, you used the revolving door. If you wanted the restaurant you used the lift. To enter the restaurant, we followed the instructions on the wall to press a button for the lift. After a light lunch, picking off the menu what we felt comfortable with as we negotiated our way around the menu, we did not linger after eating.

The student gathering was much noisier as we re-entered the square; not lingering as we quietly passed but deciding to go with haste back to the railway station and make our way back to Giardini Naxos.

Our return journey on the train gave us a different aspect of the rocky coast. Leaving the station, the train passed by many railway tracks along which moved much rolling stock. A testament to the workday life of this busy port. A group of young people entertained us on the train; one of them tapped away on his bongo drums. As the train slowed down at one or two stations such as Ali Terme, there was a quick glimpse of other towns along the way.

'We are getting quite near to Taormina now,' I told myself as I saw a fort on top of a hill which overlooked a bay of the Ionian Sea. I filmed it all. Again, I saw the rocky outcrops which I learned some years later was at Mazzaro just below Taormina.

'We are coming into the station now.' The buildings of Giardini Naxos came into view along the coast. 'It is time to catch the bus back to our hotel.'

'Here we are.' My husband called me back to reality from where I was catching the view of the outside of this wonderful railway station. Soon we were speeding by bus through the narrow streets of Giardini old town to the other side. The views gave way to a glimpse of palm trees lining the sea front. Returning to our hotel in the setting sun, I filmed one last time the tranquil scene of the boats in the harbour.

Later that evening, with the aid of my newly purchased map we happily planned. A possible journey through Italy to Sicily? Just us two? What excitement.

We had enjoyed today's adventure into the unknown, reflecting that all things are possible if only you know how. It is the fear of the unknown that stops us pushing back the boundaries and trying something new.

Syracuse.

An excursion to Syracuse [Sicilian spelling] was not to be missed. Planned for a Friday, the day dawned with the church bells across the bay again ringing at sunrise, bidding us to wake and greet the day before collecting our packed lunch ready for the day to unfold. We knew that it would be a long day but also that there would be an opportunity for free time where we could relax at leisure.

The ancient Greek city of Syracuse lies on the coast, more towards the south of the island, in the Gulf of Catania.

"The city is notable for its rich Greek history, culture, amphitheatres, architecture, and as the birthplace of the preeminent mathematician and engineer Archimedes." (Wikipedia.)

Our journey took us straight down the coast road, passing the city of Catania before turning seawards to our destination. Our guide explained to us where to find the main sights if we were wandering off on our own; the layout of the small island from where we could take a boat ride after she had given us a guided tour of the city; how we could find our bearings to make our way back to the bus pick-up point; finally, to let her know if we were to break away from the main group so that she would not be searching for missing people.

The coach driver took us on a short tour of the city where we saw row upon row of tall, imposing buildings rising high into the sky. The creamy stonework was enhanced by wrought iron balconies which adorned most of the windows. Down below at street level modern day cars were packed nose to tail as they found a parking space. The tour took us to the sea front where yachts bobbed lazily in the harbour and parked cars lined the waterside in happy confusion with scooters. In the distance, tall skyscraper buildings gave us a glimpse of a more modern-day Syracuse.

Leaving the coach, the official city guide welcomed us all to Syracuse. Being somewhat younger than most of the party, our official dedicated guide – not the one on the coach – walked a little too fast for others with walking difficulties. Such was the determination of a few, who were possibly re-visiting places where they had served in the Second World War [1939-45], that they overcame all obstacles and with the aid of walking sticks soldiered on, eventually catching up with the main group. Crossing one of the two bridges which connect it to the mainland, we were now on the ancient Isola di Ortygia (Island of Ortygia). This is the historic centre of Syracuse and where you will also find many shops.

The November day was bathed in warm Sicilian sunshine. It was so pleasant. The hustle and bustle of modern day traffic and the noisy scooters mixed with the ancient history of our surroundings and the main sights. Can't you just imagine the ways of transport in days gone by?

One of the highlights of the tour was the Cathedral or Duomo with its Baroque façade. This was our first stop and lesson. The Cathedral was on one side of a huge, long piazza, which was very noisy as hammering, banging and shouts rendered the air. Much restoration work was going on with workers beavering industrially behind the green netting covering the parts of building being worked on. I meanwhile, broke away from the main group to wander around the huge piazza, peering through massive doorways into the courtyards and interiors of the buildings beyond.

Gathering outside the massive ancient doors of this immense edifice, our guide explained the history of this beautiful building which started life as a Greek Temple. Originally made up of columns on four sides, it later became a Roman temple when larger pillars were built around these Greek pillars. Later again, they were filled in to make walls as it became a church.

I returned to the party from my impromptu exploration of the piazza and entered with everyone else, the interior of the Cathedral. It was still possible to touch and feel these original Greek pillars and hard to comprehend the age of the building. After meandering around the coolness of the interior inside, with most of our time there in a state of complete awe, we returned to the heat and blazing sunshine outside.

Following our guide, we continued down narrow streets that were adorned with washing and plants hanging from a profusion of balconies. Balconies on buildings which had survived for hundreds of years. On the way, our guide pointed out the site of archaeological remains which we visited briefly to allow a photo opportunity.

With time for us to wander at will and eat our packed lunch that the hotel had provided, there was an option to take a boat ride into the harbour and around the island. I, of course, jumped at this opportunity. Allen meanwhile, was more than happy to stay on terra firma and enjoy his lunch sitting on a bench under the trees by the waterside.

The boat was an old one. By 'old', I mean 'old', very old and in fact almost a wonder that it was still in use. Leaving the shore, I could appreciate the full beauty of the architecture; it was easy to understand why they called it 'Little Venice' as the tall buildings facing the sea were of Venetian style – a contrast to what we had just seen. The boat clanked and rattled its way around the bay to the old fort at the far end that had guarded the city from the enemy in days gone by. With much noisy clanking of the engine we arrived back to base without breaking down.

Arriving back on land, I met up with Allen whom meanwhile, had had a high old time simply strolling around, enjoying the sunshine, and generally watching the world go by Making our way back to the meeting point, an astonishing sight met our eyes.

'Well, here we are back in Syracuse and what do we see but a London Bus.' [For the camcorder]

It was an old, red, London Bus with a sign proclaiming that it was bound for – or had come from – Tottenham Court Road Station. (I think *not*.)

'Well I never, I wonder what it is doing here,' I mused to myself.

The bus appeared to be well-preserved with a fancy cover on the roof. No doubt it was open-topped and the cover was to shade passengers from the sun as the ones in Valencia.in Spain do. Huge letters proclaiming BUS were painted on the side of the bus in-between the top and bottom decks. A concertina-like gate secured the platform – the type that you used to see on a lift/elevator in a store or tube station. You do see the most unexpected sights sometimes and this one certainly was unexpected and quite incongruous amidst all this history and culture of an ancient Greek city. We just had to capture this on film.

A RED LONDON BUS IN SYRACUSE.

It was getting late in the afternoon and we were far from home but the day was not over. Returning to the hotel, we were to stop on the way at another historical sight which was rather taxing this late in the day.

Firstly, though, we passed the temple that was built over the Weeping Madonna, and the Greek Theatre before we arrived at the excavations, the Amphitheatre and the Ear of Dionysius.

http://www.catholictradition.org/Mary/syracuse.htm

Our guide warned us that there was quite a lot of walking involved in this leg of the journey. I, not being the most agile of persons, elected to sit on a wall outside and simply enjoy the air. Allen, ever keen to see as much as possible when it comes to ancient history, followed the group. he took some photos of all these but the most fascinating, for me at least, was the Ear of Dionysius.

This is a cave with excellent acoustics built into the rock, the entrance of which is shaped like an ear. It was possible to go right inside the 'ear' which Allen of course did. He came back full of all that he had seen. I must say that archaeological remains do not really excite me but we both had a wonderful time doing what we enjoyed best.

The final leg of the journey back to the hotel was uneventful apart from a sombre moment when we passed the War Cemetery. Passing rows upon rows of white grave headstones in a rigid formation, we came to a stop as one or two of our party wanted to visit the graves of loved ones who were buried there. It was nearly Remembrance Sunday and a sombre timely reminder of the sacrifices made by so many as we reflected how our own history was bound with that of Sicily.

Giardini Naxos.

A visit to a new town is not complete without a visit to the local market. Our Rep. informed us that this was held on a Sunday and was within easy walking distance from the hotel. I think he was having a laugh. Following the directions that we had been given and assured were correct, we turned right, out of the hotel towards the more residential part. On and on we went, wondering how much further we would have to walk in the heat. It was truly warm, reaching seventy degrees Fahrenheit. Eventually, after about two miles we came, dusty and weary, to the market. One market is much the same as another but there is this compulsion for many to visit when in a new town. After a quick wander down the rows of stalls, we set off for the lengthy walk back in the increasing heat, thankful to reach our hotel for lunch. I don't recall that we ever found the bus that we had been promised went to market.

Although not a 'shopper' in the true sense of the word, we do like to wander around the shops, especially in such a traditional town such as Giardini Naxos. A little way from the hotel was a boutique. With nose pressed to the window, I feasted my eyes on a gold coloured evening bag which was on display. Shaped like a boat, it was covered in a pattern of sequins. We eventually went into the shop and bought it for my Christmas present.

Another day, we wandered further into the older part of Giardini Naxos. The buildings here were unremarkable being built into quite plain streets. They looked quite poor but that was just the outside as inside, through an open door the very clean and modern decor was visible. A funeral procession came around the corner. Many black-suited dark-haired men escorted the hearse as it took the occupant to its final resting place.

Venturing down another street, I noticed a shoe shop – well I have to, haven't I? – with a SALE sign in the window. The stock was mainly boots. It was that time of year when locals took to their boots and warm coats even though tourists were in short sleeves. The new stock was mainly made up of knee-high boots. We notice that fashions abroad are a couple of years ahead of the UK. There was, however, a pair of high-heeled ankle boots at a greatly discounted price. Entering the shop, I asked to try them on. The leather was so very soft and what is more, the lining was one complete piece of the softest leather you could imagine. At sixty Euros, we could not leave them on the shelf. I must note that they would have cost much more in the UK and, considering that over ten years later I am still wearing them with new soles and heels at regular intervals, they work out at less than ten

GBP a year. I keep looking for a new pair but decide against it as I have not seen the like of this pair again. Perhaps another visit to Giardini Naxos? In another shop, I tried on a two-piece leisure outfit. I am still wearing the zip jacket.

The hotel was blessed with a 'sun roof' where guests could relax and soak up the sunshine. It was hot enough in November on this visit. It must be unbearable in the height of summer.

Leaving Giardini Naxcos for the airport on this visit, we had a glimpse of Mount Etna 'smoking'. Thankfully there were no eruptions while we were there. Remember, Mount Etna is an active volcano.

******

Some years later . . .

One bright day in September 2011, we found ourselves at our Gatwick airport hotel. The telephone rang.

'We are in Gatwick actually,' Allen laughed as he listened carefully to the voice at the other end. and put the phone down.

'That was Saga,' he called to me where I was exploring the spacious bathroom in the hotel. 'They don't have a room in Sicily.'

'Oh no,' was my first thought, 'Sicily was the reason for the trip.'

As I kept calm and looked disbelievingly at him, he ventured, warily gauging my reaction,

'The hotel is full and we are now staying at a sister hotel about thirty kilometres nearer to the coast.' Oh, he *is* naughty.

Now, arriving in Sicily after a wonderful tour of Puglia, Basilicata, and Calabria in the very foot of the long leg of Italy we have travelled across the Straits of Messina which lie between the toe of Italy and Sicily.

******

Renzo, our driver, moved off and carefully drove down the ramp of the ferry. I eagerly scanned the side of the quayside wondering if we would see what had truly amazed us in 2005.

'Oh, look,' I exclaimed. 'That is where that man was sitting on the ground, feet over the side, with his fishing rods trying to catch fish.'

A laugh from my husband was the answer.

It was clear that we were now in the rush hour as we ploughed our way through the centre of the city to reach the motorway above to take us to Taormina. There were so many memories now of when we had made the journey by train to Messina from Giardini Naxos to see how the land lay in the ferry port if we were able to come on the Gold Wing trike. There had been a student demonstration then and, as we waited to cross the road, a passer-by had admonished me to 'put that away', as she pointed to the camcorder slung around my neck.

Now, eagerly looking forward to our stay near Taormina we both reflected,

'I wonder what our hotel will be like.'

As we ended our journey through to the very tip of the long leg of Italy, we were not to know what a gift awaited us on our latest island interlude.[i]

As the hotel change was extremely last minute, we didn't have any details of exactly where it was situated or what the facilities were. Renzo negotiated the hustle and bustle of Messina to join the motorway. This ran very close to the sea so we had glimpses of the area.

Eventually, he turned off the motorway onto the narrow coast road.

Eagerly, we all waited in anticipation as the coach pulled up outside a hotel which was fronting the pavement. Behind we could see the glistening sea. As the entrance was narrow and limited with no room for our driver to turn around, we had to leave the coach quickly with our hand luggage and go down the path into the hotel to check in. Hotel staff gathered to unload our luggage quickly, allowing Renzo to move off in the limited time allowed to a place where he could park up safely.

Entering the hotel, we wondered about the layout as it appeared that we were on the top floor. However, we were in fact on the fourth floor with all the other levels cascading down the rocky cliff face fronting the sea. Our fears of a raw deal were dissipated. This was wonderful. Our rooms were very plush with very ornate light fittings. Patio doors opened onto a balcony facing the sea. Steps led down from the balcony to the beach but found that we were content to relax in the sunshine and drink in the tranquil view. The rocks jutting out into the sea which we had seen from Taormina and the train on our earlier visit were there – in front of us. Behind the rocks a huge yacht lay at rest.

After our long journey, we were thirsty so I went in search of something cool to drink. On the reception floor, many rooms led off a corridor. They appeared to be exclusive. Eventually, I located a barman who insisted that he would bring drinks to us in our room. I could not find a bar for instant service.

Back on our balcony a knock at the door alerted us to a visitor whereupon a very smart waiter came in with our drinks which he served with a flourish. Signing the bill – it had to be charged to our room – we settled down to relax.

On looking at the bill we felt a big hole being made in our pocket. For a gin and tonic and a can of diet cola it was about thirteen Euros. Well, that settled that. We couldn't afford to drink there. Although there was wine with dinner, we were on half board [breakfast and dinner] at this hotel and all manner of refreshment, be it tea, coffee, water, or something stronger, would make the hole rapidly appearing in our pocket, bigger. Not to mention the cost of lunch in the hotel. We needed to do a reccae of the area.

After a short rest, we explored the hotel to get our bearings and ask for a map. Leaving the hotel, we strolled around, crossing the road to the little shop we had noticed to buy a large bottle each of Cola, water, and a bottle of wine. We also noticed that they sold food.

The restaurant at the Grand Hotel Sea Palace Mazzaro certainly was as de-luxe as it proclaimed. There were not as many guests for dinner as there were for breakfast. This [breakfast] was an informal buffet affair with many guests opting to enjoy the sea air and sunshine on the terrace which led out from the restaurant. The choice of food was unbelievable with every need or desire catered for.

At dinner, we had the opportunity to choose our table and settled for sitting with many of the guests who had been our companions earlier in the tour. On the first evening we were treated to a choice of zuppa di funghi (mushroom soup), formaggi con pere e miele (cheese with pear and honey), or risotto al parmigiano (risotto with parmesan) for a first course; prosciutto di parma e mozzarella (parma ham and mozzarella), pesce spada con capperi e salsa al pomodoro (swordfish with capers and tomato sauce), or petto di poll con bacon (chicken breast with bacon) all accompanied by patate bollite (boiled) and verdura grigliate (grilled vegetables) for the main course. It was hard to choose between cannolo siciliano [Italian pastry dessert of Sicily], macedonia di frutta (fruit salad), or gelato (ice cream) for dessert; all washed down with still or sparkling water, Barbazzale Bianco, or Rosso (white or red) wine.

The second evening was just as good with a choice of zuppa di porri (leek soup), pennette al pesto (pasta with pesto), or asparagi grigliati con bacon (grilled asparagus with bacon) for the first course; for the main course a choice of parmigiana di melanzane (aubergine with eggplants), roast beef con salsa gravy (roast beef with gravy), or spigola in umido con salsa di pomodoro (stewed seabass with tomato sauce) all accompanied with baked potatoes and boiled vegetables. We were then tempted by a choice of frutta fresca (fresh fruit), semifreddo di mandorle (almond parfait), or fragole con panna e cioccolato (fresh strawberries with cream and chocolate) for dessert. With a choice (or both) of Chardonnay Patria or Nero d'Avola Patria and mineral water, we were replete.

The itinerary for Sicily included optional excursions to Mount Etna and Syracuse. The original hotel would have been on the slopes of Mount Etna and we would either have possibly joined the trip or made our way to Taormina on our own if that was a feasible option.

However, we had landed in the most perfect place to spend a few days. The cable car station to Taormina was literally two minutes away; family caring pressures were increasing and we needed to draw breath and re-connect; we had already been to Syracuse. There was no contest. Our time here was so short and we wanted to explore Taormina in greater detail. We therefore decided to simply chill out and wander at will. It was a good decision.

The following day, we took the cable car to Taormina. It soared slowly up the hillside, over the football field, and came to rest in the town. It was but a short walk to the centre of town where we re-visited places that we had explored before. We did not go to the Greek Theatre gain but we did wander in that direction as we had thoughts of buying one of those intricate metal figures from the shop near the Greek Theatre. In the end, I could not make up my mind and they did seem a bit expensive for our pockets. I admired the pottery in the shop as well but the novelty had worn off and we came away empty handed.

Strolling around we came again to the huge piazza by the Cathedral which overlooks the sea. Entering one of the churches we found out the times of Sunday Mass and made a note of all the options and different churches. As the sun was getting hotter in the September day, we returned to the cable car station and back to Mazzaro. Here we visited the little shop again and with sign language and limited Italian we came away with a huge, what we call a, 'bap or barm cake'. This huge, flat, round-shaped bread roll was filled with ham and salad. The lady obligingly cut it into two as it was large enough to share. We also bought fruit and tomatoes. Taking this feast back to our room, we settled down on the balcony to devour this wonderfully fresh bread with ham salad, all washed down with a cool drink of choice.

It was tempting to make our way down the flights of steps to the beach set in a sheltered and private cove but in the end decided that we were too lazy and were better saying on the balcony in the shade.

On looking at the map of Taormina, we had noticed various paths which wound down from the top to the main road below. The following day, Saturday, we again made our way to the cable car station for the journey to the top. Following the map, we walked down the road away from the town to where the steps started.

Slowly was the essence of the day. The steps were easily negotiated. They were shallow with a long stretch between each one. With many stops to admire the view we came to a spot with huge boulders at the side. Allen sat on one with a sheer drop down into the sea below. Well, it would have been a very bumpy drop but he was careful.

I couldn't help but reflect that this view had probably not changed in hundreds if not thousands of years. It certainly was back to nature as everything else was stripped back. And not only a return to nature, but a return to the things that really matter, putting daily cares and tribulations into perspective.

In the blistering heat; in this tranquil and peaceful corner of God's beautiful world where the unimagined views from every corner were different; in this peaceful corner where birds fluttered about and where lizards lay on a wall sleeping in the sunshine; a sense of peace and comfort stole into our hearts – and healed us.

Moving on down the steps we laughingly wondered how many more there were. I felt my legs buckling as the effort sapped my strength. Eventually, the uninhabited mountainside gave way to habitation. The path became closed in as narrow alleyways came into view. All the houses were covered with a profusion of colourful flowers that spread to tumble in a glorious haphazard way over garden walls. Twisting and turning ever downwards we eventually came to the main road. Ahead was a lido and more activity. To our left was another hotel, just across the road from ours. I wasn't sure I would make it, but I staggered along and almost fell up the steps to the terrace. Never had we been so glad of a rest and cool drink. Again, we bought our picnic lunch from the little shop. With the prices in the hotel the owner had a good spot there in attracting customers.

In the evening, many of our group went to the hotel across the road where we had stopped after our trek down the mountainside and later, usually had a lively time on the terrace.

After dinner that night we did have drinks in the hotel and thought, 'Hang the cost. You only live once.' We had been spoiled with all-inclusive Saga Holidays.

Sunday dawned with clear skies and beautiful sunshine. After breakfast, we took the cable car again up to Taormina. We had decided on which church to go to even though the Mass was in Italian. We knew that we could follow it. The church was not a massive one and was crowded. The heat almost overcame some of the congregation. Afterwards we again strolled among what had become a special place for us, looking for a restaurant for Sunday lunch. We usually treat ourselves to a proper Sunday lunch if we are away and lunch is not included in the holiday price. However, as this was our last day and we had the Gala Farewell Dinner to look forward to, a light lunch was called for.

Some of the group had gone on another excursion. As it was their first time in Sicily they wanted to see as much as possible but it did mean that they did not have the opportunity to see much of Taormina and they had been on the go all the time. We can empathise with that as you always think that 'we might not come again' and so do as much as possible. Having been before we were content to just relax and explore more fully the area which drew us into its heart – and ours.

Our last evening in this luxury hotel – the end to what had been an idyllic finale to a wonderful exploration of the southern end of the unspoiled long leg of Italy and Sicily – was the occasion of our Saga Gala Farewell Dinner. We had kept to the chosen table for eight, and companions, as suggested at the outset by our tour manager. Apart from getting to know one another better, this made it easier for the waiters to serve the meal selection chosen the previous evening. On this last evening seating was freestyle meaning that we could change if we wished. Some guests gravitated to our table as they wanted a change and a slice of the vibrant conversation emanating over the air. Consequently, we lost our usual place with our pleasant dining companions with whom we had enjoyed some lively and wide-ranging conversations. Although not a problem, in itself, as it was nice to chat to other members of the group, it did mean that the waiters were serving the wrong meals to the tables. However, all was sorted and we looked forward to our last dinner of the tour. this meal was a four-course meal.

The first course gave us a choice of Selezione di vedure con fonduta di formaggio (vegetables selection with cheese fondue), or polpette di manzo con salsa di pomodoro fresco (beef meatballs with fresh tomato sauce). We both chose the meatballs.

The second course offered a choice of zuppa di asparagi (asparagus soup), risotto con erbe aromatiche (risotto with aromatic herbs), or lasagna (lasagne) – which we both chose.

Taking a deep breath and making room for the third course we had perused the choice of: involtini di verdura con mollica (rolled vegetables breadcrumbs) [translations from the menu], agnello arrosto (roast lamb) which Allen chose, pesce San Pietro grigliato con salsa di cipolla rossa (grilled San Pietro fish with red onion sauce) which was my choice, accompanied by patate al forne (baked potatoes) [Allen], or insalata fresca (fresh salad) [me] for this main course. As usual, le acque oligominerali (still or sparkling mineral water), was on hand to wash it all down. The red and white wines this evening were Etna Bianco Patria and Etna Rosso Patria. Just when we thought that we could not manage anymore food, the waiters brought out cake or torta.

Our tour manager reminded us of the arrangements for the morrow before Allen and I repaired to the bar lounge for a quiet night-cap. It was pleasant to sit quietly and look back upon, not only the whole experience, but the last few days in this idyllic corner of the world which had given us such contentment and healing. Looking up towards the ceiling as we slid lower and lower in our chairs, we were treated to a view of decorative panel of glass in the ceiling through which light shone. Others of our group met up again in the hotel across the way where they had another riotous evening on the terrace in the cooling Sicilian air.

They *did* all make it down to breakfast the following morning. Just as well as we were to leave quite soon afterwards. With cases packed, I wandered out onto the balcony. I kept popping in and out as I sorted my belongings. I could not drink in enough of the view from the balcony with its partitions topped with wrought iron and urns of flowers, the outcrops of rock in the sea; the rows of sun loungers shaded by umbrellas on the beach below waiting patiently for its occupants. Who would they be today? A view which again seemed timeless.

With one last look around our luxurious room, we memorised the intricacies of the ornate wall lights; the wall sconces made up of bunches of grapes and vine leaves in shades of green and gold which held the uplifted lamp shades. As in our room, the whole hotel was enriched with very solid wood panelling and doors. The walls were hung with glorious framed pictures while in the dining room, the low-ceiling supported large chandeliers of the same style as the wall lights in our room. Everywhere, luxury was evident.

With our flight being in the late afternoon and hotel checkout in the morning, our tour manager had to find something to occupy us for the day. Renzo, our driver, seemed to have relations everywhere; another 'cousin' offered us lunch in their restaurant on the seafront in Giardini Naxos. Even better, we could stay for as long as we liked.

As it happened, the rain bucketed down changing any plans to explore the area. When the rain flooded down the street, the owners wound the sides of the awnings down to protect us from the wet and chill as we all feasted on fine Sicilian fare and quaffed Sicilian wine. What a contrast to the brilliant sunshine which had been caressing our skin and soothing our souls.

This lovely town by the sea was where the mystery and romance of Sicily all started for us – we did not mind the weather but spent some time reminiscing.

'Down there is the shop where we my bought boat-shaped, gold-beaded and sequinned evening bag. Over there is the hotel where we stayed.'

All the memories came back and we felt as if we had come home. Even though the sea mist and rain meant that we couldn't see far beyond the beach to the coast beyond, or indeed go on the planned boat trip, a return to an idyllic part of this island nestling timelessly in the Ionian Sea of the Mediterranean certainly rounded off what was the end of a most wonderful adventure in the very long and diverse leg of Italy and Sicily.

~~~~~~

Malta

Another day, another place, another island. What is it that draws us to the islands with their varied history, cultures, and geographical interests? Is it because we are from an island race? Whatever – we are drawn.

In June 2006, desperate for sunshine and relaxation once again from the stresses of life, we took ourselves off for our own 'Malta Experience'. Although we had some indication of what to expect from the excursions provided by Saga Holidays, the history, culture, and sheer beauty of the towns, which sat among the dusty countryside of this small and brave island bowled us over. I say 'brave' as it was almost destroyed during the Second World War Holding fast, it rose again as it, especially Valletta, was eventually re-built.

You will find many excellent websites and DVD's with more information on the culture, music festivals, fireworks festivals, outdoor, and underwater activities than I can cover here.

For example, *http://www.visitmalta.com.*

Indeed, that is not the purpose of this book. It is not a guide book per se. It is simply a traveller's account where I simply wish to share our own experiences and perhaps encourage you to push back one day your own boundaries to explore this small island. An island that lies deep in the warm waters of the Mediterranean Sea between Sicily and the North African coast. Other islands of the archipelago to visit are Gozo and Comino.

Although we expected and, indeed welcomed, a lot of sun and warmth, we did not expect the draining enervating heat of forty degrees Celsius. It was even too hot for the locals. We found that the hotel in St. Julian's Bay was newly re-furbished and exclusive to the guests of our holiday company.

As I write, I am looking again at the extensive video that I recorded of things that interested me or caught my eye; the many photographs that my husband took as he clicked away to capture things that interested him. Combined, they make a comprehensive record of this adventurous escape to the sun.

St Julian's Bay is on the north-eastern side of the island. From our location at the tip of Spinola Bay, which is tucked away in a corner of the larger St. Julian's Bay, we had a view across the water towards Sliema and Valletta beyond. Each morning we listened to the sound of church bells ringing as they heralded the dawning of another day, calling to us to wake up and explore this fascinating island.

Capturing the early morning scene across the bay one Saturday morning, I am heard to share my thoughts.

'It is eight o'clock on Saturday morning. The church bells have just rung across the bay. We are in St. Julian's Bay on the north coast of Malta. It promises to be another hot day. I think that yesterday it must have touched forty degrees Celsius.

Yesterday afternoon, several beautiful boats sailed into the harbour. We have a contrast of the very traditional fishing boats which are over there, [I zoomed in to the other side of the bay, panning the camera around to the colourful blue and yellow fishing boats] and the very modern, smooth yachts.'

I continued with more shots of the bay.

'The hotel is perched on the corner of St. Julian's Bay and the sea.' I panned around from my vantage point on our balcony to an inviting view of the pool down below. 'Because of our room location, we have a view of both. As the sun is so strong at eight o'clock, I can't get a view as, if I film into the sun, I will crack the lens [camcorder] or something direr. The hotel is brand new. It opened in September and it is excellent.'

As I changed my position on the balcony, I was able to capture a very modern sight of Portomaso Marina with the beautiful white yachts sleeping in the early morning sunshine.

It is time now to explore.

Qormi.

In the southern region of Malta, Qormi is known by its title Citta Pinto. It is the fifth largest city of Malta and has two Parishes – the Parish of St. George and the second one the Parish of St. Sebastian. My Maltese friend/colleague who shared this information, was born, lived, and was married in Qormi.

The first part of today's adventure was a visit to a typical farmhouse and a talk about the island. The farmhouse was not like any that we had seen before. The rooms were built around a central courtyard. Many archways led to the rooms within; the upper story was surrounded by a balcony running all around, from which hung a variety of greenery. The courtyard was laid out with long tables set out for our refreshments. As the courtyard was open to the elements, everywhere was a pleasant feeling of light and air.

After making an orderly queue to collect a cup of tea and typical Maltese cake that was set out on long tables, everyone found a seat to rest and enjoy the forthcoming talk on the area. This included how people lived and make a living from the wines and crafts made there. Afterwards, our route out to the coach took us – naturally – through the inevitable shop that sold all manner of goods including wine.

The Ta' Qali Craft Centre.

From Qormi we went into the centre of the island to visit the Ta' Qali Craft Centre. The craft centre is built on the site of an abandoned World War Two airfield. The old Nissan huts have been utilized to convert to shops. They contain all manner of authentic Maltese crafts such as jewellery, pottery, and glass to name a few. This is where the famous Mdina Glass is made and sold. You can see what interests me and, yes, I did succumb to a pair of hoop earrings in Maltese silver. They are of a quite dull silver. A rope effect of silver circles twist around the hoop that is decorated with a coral colour along the bottom. Due to weight restrictions on luggage, I unfortunately had to forgo pottery and glassware. One pottery that we went into was the Bristow Pottery. I entreated my husband to take a snap as, at the time, I worked with a colleague with the surname of Bristow.

The journey back to the hotel took us along wide and leafy roads lined with imposing buildings. The mellow stonework glistened in the sunshine; an abundance of flags fluttered in the breeze, their gold and red cloth adding an exotic air to our surroundings. Deep in the countryside where flowering shrubs and greenery lined the roads, the city of Mdina was clearly visible in the distance as it rose above the surrounding flat land. This exploration was for another day. Our focus now was to get back to our hotel for a welcome rest on our balcony.

Around St. Julian's Bay.

St. Julian's Bay on the north coast of Malta, is the larger bay enhanced by smaller bays that follow the contours of the coastline. We were based at the tip of Spinola Bay with the sights and sounds of Sliema in front of us. Later that afternoon I continued recording.

'There are quite a few boats on the horizon. I am not sure if you can see them from here [on the film].'

I was then able to capture St. Julian's Tower that sits at the tip of land jutting out from Sliema and the many tall buildings that line the shore. Beyond that, the sailors taking advantage of the sunshine and coolness out on the water as they sailed their yachts in full sail. Of course, not everyone was so energetic. Many sleek motor launches and yachts were still sleeping peacefully. One boat was towing a smaller one behind, no doubt for getting closer to shore. As it was the middle of a major football tournament – don't expect me to know what it was or who was playing – there was a lot of cheering across the bay that even my family could hear when I telephoned them later.

I observed that,

'It is now coming to the end of the afternoon. It has been quite a peaceful if long day.'

It was far too hot to walk to Sliema so we opted to take the shuttle bus, thoughtfully provided by the hotel for the comfort of guests, up the long hill and then stroll back down to the hotel. We made frequent stops to admire the view of the marina across the bay (behind our hotel) and the typical Maltese fishing boats in the sea. These were brightly coloured and moored comfortably among the more modern boats and cruisers.

The new marina was a magnet for a quiet stroll to admire the luxurious cruisers moored in front of the newly built apartments. Our evenings were spent on the hotel terrace by the water's edge, listening to music and sounds from across the bay – not least the cheering of football fans when the World Cup matches were playing on TV and the locals gathered in the bars to watch and support their favourite team.

Another evening, filming on the terrace.

'It is Tuesday and the sun has set. It will soon be an inky, black sky so I am taking this opportunity to take a picture of the bay.'

I panned the camcorder around to show how different everything looks with the lights shining on the water and the sounds of chatter and laughter in the background.

'It is extremely hot here. It is thirty-six/thirty-seven degrees Celsius, nearly a hundred degrees Fahrenheit altogether.'

With the chink of cutlery and crockery behind me on the upper terrace where diners enjoy the evening air, I continued recording.

'They say St. Julian's Bay is called Spinola Bay. It is a long, narrow bay. Over the weekend, it was full of motor launches and yachts, which have all gone away now. At the other side of the hotel is a marina with many yachts and boats. Some are moored seemingly permanently. The setting is perfect. Fabulous.'

Down below on the pool terrace, many palm trees for shade interspersed the sun loungers now wait for the morning visitors.

'Oh, look, one of the boats all lit up. I wonder if I can catch that.' Panning in, 'There we are, just a little behind the tree.'

The boat appeared to be a small one, quite a contrast from the elegant and majestic yachts that pepper the bay.

'Allen has gone to listen to the lecture on wartime Malta. But I opted out of that one. I am on one of the terraces listening to *Dusty Road*.'

'The boat there with the lights, can I catch it or have I wandered?'

I continued to pan around the bay, catching the reflections in the water of all the water's edge buildings, bars, etc.

'The light on the front of the boat, the fishing boat, is supposed to be the evil eye or to ward off evil. I am not sure. I will have to ask *his nibs* [husband] when he comes back,' I recorded.

In fact, as I was later informed while writing this, it was a traditional Maltese deep-sea fishing boat called a Luzzu. Luzzu has a pair of eyes at the bow which are referred to as the 'Eye of Horus or Osiris' to protect the fishermen while at sea. A Maltese boat without the 'EYE' is called a Dghajsa. A Dghajsa is a Maltese gondola, a harbour boat or a water taxi used by sailors for cutting across the creeks.

Continuing filming the bay, I commented, 'Tonight it is very warm again. We have had a lovely quiet day in the hotel, a lovely air-conditioned hotel and we have had so much sun these last two days that we thought a day inside would be good for us.'

Now I could see another fishing boat, more clearly this time, with the light on the prow. Being dark, the wonderful colours of yellow and blue were not visible.

'Tomorrow, we are going to take the shuttle bus, which is free, into Valletta and have a wander around. It will be very welcome to be collected from the hotel as the walk just up the street, to the bus stop over there [panning around the bay] is a little bit further than you think; not too bad really but when it is very, very hot it is just more than you want to do.'

Incongruously, on the skyline behind the many modern and older buildings, I could clearly see a huge crane lying still and silent with its very long arm jutting out into the black sky.

Fascinating Valletta.

'We are now in Valletta.'

A horse-drawn carriage was patiently waiting by an archway for customers – a good way to get around the city. Well, the horse was waiting patiently. The horse-drawn carriages are called 'Karozzin' which was the Maltese traditional mode of transport.

Our first impression of the city was how mellow and untouched the buildings looked. We learned that after the bombing and destruction during the Second World War where it was almost razed to the ground, it was rebuilt to look like its former self.

On the bus, we had turned in towards the sea, passing through Floriana before reaching Valletta. Valletta juts out from the coast with many creeks and bays on either side. It is a fortress city and 'built on the rock of Mount Sciberras Peninsula, which rises steeply from two deep harbours; the Marsamxett Harbour and the Grand Harbour.' *http://www.visitmalta.com/en/valletta*

FASCINATING VALLETTA.

A triple archway led to the busy streets of the city. Strolling through the Valletta City Gate a banner on an archway proclaimed:

VALLETTA. Belt ta' Patrimonju Dinji

A World Heritage City.

Valletta Rehabilitation Project.

The Triton Fountain is found at the entrance of the city gate. As we came into the huge square and dodging the many cars and people, we slowly made our way past the bus terminus to the other end of the long street towards the sea where we found a host of contrasts.

A traditional horse-drawn carriage passed a building with a huge M sign for MacDonald's restaurant. Another contrast was a church with many twisting steps rising at the side from the pavement. Many colourful flags flew in the breeze from the lovely mellow buildings. Some [churches] were very ornate with statues set high up over the doors.

Their steps provided welcome relief as a place of rest for worn-out tourists.

As time was short we didn't explore as much as we would have liked to but contented ourselves with simply absorbing some of the history and beauty of the city. St John's Co-Cathedral was one of the sights that we simply just gazed at as we wilted in the heat.

One thing we did learn however was the history of the Maltese Cross that is the emblem of Malta. Wikipedia tells us that,

"In the 15th century, the eight points of the four arms of the later called Maltese Cross represented the eight lands of origin, or 'Langues' of the 'Knights Hospitaller': Auvergne, Provence, France, Aragon, Castile and Portugal, Italy, Germany, and England (with Scotland and Ireland)." It is often depicted as black and white or red and white.

The Maltese Cross was formally adopted by the Knights Hospitallers of St. John in 1126."

http://www.maltauncovered.com/sourced 28.03.2016

Malta also has the George Cross which was awarded by King George VI in 1942 in recognition of the heroic struggle against occupation in World War II. Malta was called the 'Island Fortress' by King George VI.

Allen of course, wanted to look in the War Museum. This he found very interesting. It was also very cool. Coming out by the water's edge, we wandered around the edge of the fort before making our way back to the bus stop for the journey back to our hotel.

To Mosta and Mdina.

Included excursions to Mosta and the walled city of Mdina filled another day and took us once again into the centre of the island into the countryside. We had the opportunity to see the famous church in **Mosta**. Famous because, during the war with bombs raining down, one had gone through the domed roof.

The church is built along the lines of the Pantheon in Rome. (As we had visited there [Rome] many years ago, we can testify to that.) From the outside, we could see that the main part of the church is square but with some curved walls. Tall pillars frame the entrance through extremely tall, panelled doors. Above, twin towers flank the rotunda with a dome towering above that rises from the middle of the main part of the church.

Inside, all is light and colour. Around the perimeter are many altars in alcoves framed by richly decorated arches. The pale coloured walls, framed by white pillars, are a contrast to the otherwise rich decoration. On the high altar, I had never seen such tall candlesticks and candles that, due to the sheer scale of the church, were not out of place but perfectly balanced.

Our guide told us some of the features of this famous church that we should not miss. Craning our necks, we could see the richly decorated embossed squares in the inside of the dome. We could also see the damage to the inside of the dome where the bomb had come through during a service; at the time, the church was packed with worshippers. Miraculously, it did not explode as it landed on the ground amidst the congregation of about three hundred people; no one was killed. If you look carefully, you can pick out the exact spot, the exact square that was repaired after the bomb fell through. In the Sacristy, we saw a replica. It was huge and inconceivable that it did not explode. Truly a miracle. The Sacristy also had display cabinets of very old vestments, a model of the church. There is also a photograph of the hole in the dome where the bomb had pierced it.

Mdina is known as the Silent City. It is a walled city and ancient capital of Malta, rising high above the ground. Approaching, you can see it from a distance in the dusty plains around. Outside the walls that are topped by statues, there was the inevitable but informative tourist guide waiting for customers. This one was offering a ride in a horse-drawn carriage. In contrast to the age of the city, the guide was very modern with a relaxed dress of shorts and shirt topped by a baseball cap to protect him from the strong sunshine. Entering the fortified city through an elaborately decorated archway, our official guide took us on a short tour to point out the main historical sights of interest.

As I have said earlier, this is not a complete guide to Malta – I could not do any justice to that. This is an account of our own impressions from earlier notes, video and of course, the inevitable map. I have checked facts but to explore further you can go to http://www.visitmalta.com.

To continue our exploration from afar, I am again re-visiting our own video. I can see that these old buildings and palaces were set of with much greenery waving in the breeze and tall ornate street lamps. In front of the

Archbishop's Palace stood a sleek black car. No number plate. Just his coat of arms. A bell tower of the same mellow stone as the cathedral adorned either end at the front of the building. Some of the buildings had ornate curved grilles over the windows. A cannon set near one building had provided welcome rest for one of our group as the guide continued her talk. From the ramparts, as you walked around them you could see for miles around, across the island.

Armed then with some local knowledge so that we wouldn't get lost, we were soon able to stroll around on our own among the mellow stone of the buildings that have stood the test of time. It really was very hot and Allen was thankful for a cool drink in the shade of an outside cafe.

The excursions provided by Saga Holidays, many of which were included, as usual gave us a comprehensive overview of what the island had to offer; its history; combined with a good hotel and facilities, made an enjoyable holiday.

A cruise around the Grand Harbour of Valletta.

However, there was one thing that for me was a 'must do'. I was anxious to go on the Harbour Cruise; Allen was not keen as, and I have said this before, he can barely look at a wave poor man. One Saturday, we hopped on the shuttle bus to Sliema where we bought my ticket for another adventure. Leaving Allen behind to wander at will around Sliema and the many shops or simply sit and watch the world go by, I settled myself with a good vantage point on the boat to tour the Grand Harbour of Valletta.

I had not expected the harbour to be so big. It is enormous and gives a different dimension to all that I had heard previously. The guide, speaking over a microphone, explained that we would be cruising around the two main harbours of Marsamxett Harbour and the Grand Harbour.

The boat cruised first around Manoel Island before making its way up the western side of Valletta in Marsamxett Harbour. Rounding the corner of the fort, the most wonderful view of the walls guarding the city opened before our eyes. It reminded me of the Doge's Palace in Venice with all the archways framing the covered walkways. Further on, the outsides of the walls were not so ornate. Rounding another corner, we sailed down the other side of Valletta. Here it was clear to see how packed with buildings the city was. Above it rose the dome of the Cathedral.

Reaching the bottom end of the Grand Harbour, we were treated to a fascinating account of the layout of the harbour and the history. As I said earlier, I hadn't expected the harbour to be so huge. I certainly hadn't expected to learn about or see on the other side of the peninsula on which Valletta and Floriana stand, the Three Cities of **Vittoriosa, Senglea** and **Cospicua,** or the French Creek, Dockyard Creek, and Kalkara Creek. We saw, and the guide explained to us, the various docks from commercial to Royal Navy ones, from boatyards to the British Royal Navy 'Bighi Hospital, as the boat wended its way around the Three Cities. An experience that you can only fully appreciate first hand. I will leave you dear reader to plan your own visit.

As usual, I took lots of film and only hoped that Allen, when he watched later, would not be seasick with the boat going up and down. It was quite choppy when we got into the open sea. He would have loved to take the journey, as he would have appreciated the history.

Valletta itself is lovely and very old. After all the destruction in the Second World War, it has been re-built and there is much to see which we had done earlier on a separate day.

Farewell to Malta.

All good things end. We thoroughly enjoyed our visit to Malta. We loved the island despite the sandy dust among the green fields. But as my husband has just explained, it is largely a rock of sandstone and if you try to dust in a sandpit, sand will blow. As the breeze blows across the island, there is dust but this does not detract from the sheer volume of varied experiences. It is a good place to go for history, culture, sun, sea, wonderful hotels, and a wealth of things to do – or not.

In a reflective mood on our last night, I stood on the upper terrace to capture the last of the light over the bay as the sun sank and recorded my thoughts.

'We have eaten outside tonight. This is the end of the Saga season and the start of the Maltese summer season. They have set up tables for us tonight on the pool terrace among the palm trees and given us waiter service which is very nice [romantic].

I can see the twinkling lights of lively Sliema across the bay. There is a piano playing in the background [of the hotel terrace]. On the bay side of the hotel there is a walkway from where you can walk down steps to swim in the sea.'

The pool is floodlit. I can hear the jolly tune of *Ain't She Sweet* as the pianist pounds out popular tunes.

As I watch and listen a sailing yacht slips seamlessly around the headland into the bay, its twin masts reaching into the sky. The jolly tunes being played behind me are a contrast to the silence of the sea and the bright lights of the sailing yacht shining in the dark.

Good-bye Malta.

Cyprus

The mysterious [to me] island of Cyprus basks in the sunshine of the Eastern Mediterranean Sea. One grey November day we left the chill of the UK to escape once again for the sunshine and tranquillity of a distant island. Although we had expected much better temperatures than we experienced at home, it was a pleasant surprise to find a high seventy-degree Fahrenheit warmth with the sun beating down day by day.

This was our first visit to Cyprus. We only knew what we had read about this lush and fertile country and were eager to explore. The island of Cyprus sits in the eastern Mediterranean Sea below Turkey – the gateway to Asia – east of the Greek island of Crete and west of the countries of Syria and Israel. Cyprus is a divided island with the north belonging to Turkey and the south to Greece.

Basking quietly in the warmth of the Cyprus Sea, the island holds many secrets of its ancient and colourful past that, today, blends with its more modern surroundings as many tourists flock to discover its rich history and culture or simply to soak up the sun. Perhaps both.

Our hotel in Limassol on the south of the island was a family hotel but, being November and out of the high season, was quiet. There was so much to see; with the intention of exploring as much as possible we decided to hire a car. Looking at the inevitable map which I had purchased in a nearby shop we could see that there were good roads around the island. Driving on the left –the same as in the UK – was another bonus as was a car with a right-hand drive meaning that we slipped easily into the flow of traffic from our hotel in Limassol.

Heading west to Pafos and beyond.

The smooth road out of Limassol took us towards the ancient city of Pafos on the south-west coast. There wasn't much vegetation here but the road cut through the hills through some quite long tunnels. We could see right across the island and eventually we had glimpses of the sea. Nearing Pafos the sky was a clear blue. In the distance, there was a glimpse of Aphrodite's Rock where it lay in the sea off the coast.

The approach to Pafos is delightful with flowering trees lining the road and the glimpses of the sea increasing as we headed towards the harbour.

Forewarned is forearmed and to this end I was armed with a guide book which had the ever-essential maps. Reaching the harbour, we were greeted by a busy scene as tourists thronged the area and tall ships thrust their bunting-clad masts high into the sky. To be expected, many yachts and boats of all kinds vied for space. A harbour-side cafe set the scene for enjoying a cool drink to quench our thirst as we sat to watch the comings and goings in the morning sunshine. One boat was being re-painted and repaired; many were out of the water. It was end of season maintenance time. This part of the town is the lower end called Kato Pafos and away from the commercial area higher up, reached after a stiff uphill walk.

Relaxing and chatting, we could see the ancient fort and views across to the hills. As we watched, high in the sky a parachute was coming in to land. Would it end up in the sea? But no, it was towed by a boat and rose again in the sky. All this activity kept me busy filming which, years later as I recount this adventure, I am thankful for.

Heading now towards the ancient archaeological ruins to the west of the main road we were conscious of the rising heat. Our maps showed us that one or two of the ruined houses were featuring mosaics. Wending our way along the dusty road towards this area we came across many ruins, broken white pillars, and stones among the trees. A dog barked sharply in the background. Under the cement of floors of some buildings, we could see where the most beautiful mosaics had been unearthed. How rich and vibrant the houses must have been in that time.

We came across a memorial on which was a plaque. It read:

Historical background to

AYLA KYRIAKI CHRYSOPLITISSA CHURCH.

Visit of St. Paul and St. Barnabas.

ERIC THE GOOD from 1095 RENOWNED King of Denmark died during a pilgrimage to Pafos in the year 1103. (Memorial erected in 1995.)

Wandering on we saw the remains of St. Paul's Pillar; a piece of stone where St. Paul, who visited in 45AD, was tied, and whipped with forty lashes for evangelising the island.

Allen was keen to visit the House of Dionysus to look at the mosaics and headed in the direction of the road which led to it. It was difficult to follow the road on the map. Puzzled, we stopped to check it. Where is the road? All we could see was a wide dirt track lined with trees as if going through an orchard or park. Not a made-up road at all.

Wearing his Gold Wing hat to shade him from the sun, Allen sat on a wall to rest. (We had recently ventured into Gold Wing motorcycling touring world. Have I mentioned that before?)

Eventually, we reached our destination. The floor in the House of Dionysus – built around the end of the second century AD – I could see, was very cleverly laid out. Although the floor was flat, overall it had a 3D effect. Each panel or picture was made up of individual coloured bricks, set to form a 3D mosaic-like picture. Each panel was divided by what looked like turrets forming a wall around it. Each panel was different scene.

To preserve the relics a raised platform had been erected as a walkway from which you could look down to what had been unearthed. The outside of the edge of the floor was filled with paintings of large animals or beasts with men fighting them.

Allen, as usual, could have spent longer examining each minute detail. *(He has checked, corrected and refined my descriptions and tells me now that he could have spent hours examining every minute detail. In fact, if I had left him, he would probably have still been there. For my part, I didn't work this hard when doing my GCE end-of-school exams in my youth.)*

Back by the harbour the colourful fishing boats were bobbing at anchor. Allen wandered over to an old green and red bus or coach. (Looking now at the video as we played it back he thought that it may have been an old

Mercedes but was not sure.) Lazily, we watched the sea slapping against the rocky shore.

Another day, with views of the sea and coast along the way, we drove high into the hills to Polis which lies in a beautiful curved bay – Chrysochou Bay – on the north-west of the island. We reached this delightful village – one which we explored in more detail on a return visit – from good roads on the greener west coast. This was only a fleeting visit. We pulled in to admire the coast and to allow me to capture the scenery on film. Although the sound on the film which I took in 2000 has become distorted in places, I was able to pick out the following,

'We are on our way back to the hotel after a day on the west coast. We have just driven down from Polis in the north-west. In front of us now is Aphrodite's Rock. This is where Aphrodite, the Greek goddess of love, is reputed to have risen from the sea at birth.'

The rocky shore here looked red as the setting sun cast a red glow across it. It was winter and the days shorter – but still hot.

Troodos Mountains.

Heading inland from Limassol, our destination today was the Troodos Mountains and a visit to the Kykkos Monastery deep in the north-west of the mountains.

Away from the excellent roads of the coast we found a great difference as we ventured north into the mountains. Many very old trucks and other vehicles contrasted with newer and smarter ones. There were also, tractors. Driving high into the hills we were treated to spectacular views across the fertile land. The road was not quite so good here – just a tarmaced section with no markings and the sides of the road left rough.

Passing through a mountain village we stopped to explore. The streets of this village were lined with smart houses. Shop fronts were adorned with displays of lace, rugs and bedspreads draped over all manner of things like chairs and a washing line. Sunshades and umbrellas protected more delicate lace. A cat, from its position at the edge of a pavement, lazily washed itself.

Down a cobbled street more shops and cafés displayed their wares (souvenirs). Some of the streets were very narrow and steep. Through archways of a courtyard sat a group of white-haired old ladies who were dressed in black and grey. They didn't seem to retire but occupied themselves industriously with lace-making. One in particular – set apart from the others where she could catch some warmth from the sun – was dressed in black with a black hairnet on her white hair, black jumper, grey skirt, thick black stockings, and black boots. She was having a laugh and a joke with another lady nearby in-between working at the lace on her lap.

Another lady put down her work altogether as she chatted to her friends who had stopped as they passed by. The building looked like a cloister type of building and they sat where the sun warmed them out of the shadows of the archways.

In fact, looking more closely at the film which I had taken, it *was* cloisters, as the next shots are of inside the richly adorned church. White walls and rich wood were complemented by elaborate candleabras. Outside, on the other side of the church, the cloisters were two storeys high with a balcony running all around.

One old house with wooden steps leading up to its entrance had a sign which proclaimed that it was 'Socrates Traditional House'. (Checking for information on this, I found that we were in Omodos, well off the beaten track. Evidently, we had not taken the direct route out of Limassol, which sounds about right as we usually say, 'let's go', and end up in all sorts of unexpected and charming places.)

The roofs over the doorways of many buildings were decorated with ripening fruit tumbling around and over them amidst the leaves of the plant while tall cypress trees in the cemetery reached up into the sky.

Continuing up the mountain roads that were increasingly bumpy and rough, the exposed rock was chalky here but all was lush and green. We rocked and rolled along the road, not quite sure of where we were heading but feeling very re-assured when we saw a white line in the road.

'Oh look. we have got a white line.' I was excited. There were also more serious fences and fence posts.

'Back to civilization,' I exclaimed.

Then, we came to the outskirts of a village. They had just taken the road up. Ahead, a digger and road roller were working on the left-hand side of the road. An oldish man was standing in the road watching for traffic. Do we stop? Do we have to turn around and go back? Passage appeared unlikely but the man simply waved us on with a smile. No STOP signs or traffic lights. We bounced along, doing as instructed, not knowing what we were to be greeted with next. On a side road, a huge tanker, coming down from the mountain, waited to slip onto the road.

Eventually, we reached the Kykkos Monastery Museum. As no photographs are allowed we bought the video. We do remember that it was an amazing experience. From the back of our tickets, which cost £1.50 (Cyprus pounds) then, I can see from the small map that the main entrance led into a large courtyard. This led into another one and then a church.

On the left of the main entrance was the ticket office and sales room. From these led a room with 'antiquities' between these last two and the courtyard. Further on from the ticket and sales rooms was an enormous room which displayed Early Christian, Byzantine, and Post-Byzantine church vestments and vessels. Also, jewels and *what* jewels. They took our breath away. A small octagonal room housed manuscripts, documents, and books while a larger octagonal room on the other side displayed icons, wall paintings, and wood carvings.

Leaving the Monastery, we stopped along the road to drink in the views from this high vantage point in the mountains. The Troodos mountains with their many different types of trees are beautiful with the most fantastic views and between the leaves of the trees, glimpses of red-roofed houses tumbling down the mountainside. The whole setting was one of coolness, tranquillity, and timelessness. This coolness was greatly appreciated after the heat of the coast.

On the way down, we saw a garage/petrol station. It sported a Honda sign and proclaimed that it was a 'Famous Garage'. The voices of children playing in a nearby school playground brought us back to reality.

Lefkara.
We had heard about the village of Lefkara with its famous lace called lefkaritiko and the silverware for which it is also famous. Heading north out of Limassol we soon came to the outskirts of the village. Turning off the main road onto a minor one I announced that,

'We are in Lefkara now and are going to park up.'

Outside the village there was a 'Stop & Look' sign for Lefkara lace and silver. Following a 'Parking' sign we turned into a narrow street where the walls were hung with beautifully embroidered tablecloths. It was one way of displaying goods. The women were again dressed in traditional black clothes.

The streets were narrow with square buildings. The walls of the buildings were either white, yellow, or simply grey stone flecked with white; some had balconies while some had shutters on their windows. Many displayed their wares outside. A familiar sight was to see a family member sitting outside a shop. Not simply sitting but hard at work on lace, embroidery or drawn thread work, stitching industriously in the sunshine while behind, a huge variety of goods tempted you inside. *(Apart from taking in the clean mountain air, sitting outside working is a way of also catching your attention. I remember years ago, when I was in direct selling and working on exhibition stands for a window firm, a sure way to attract customers was to start cleaning the windows on the stand.)*

One shop had a huge sign outside. It proclaimed,

LOUIS. Lace Workshop. Silver & Souvenir.
Branches: Wales, Midlands, Yorkshire, Teesside, Northumberland.
And taped to the bottom was a new sign for CARDIFF.

Another advertised that it belonged to,

HARRY LOIZOU. Liverpool Branch. Allerton.
Specialist in Lefkara Embroidery and Silver designs.
18carat Gold plus jewellery, souvenir, gifts.

Intrigued, we entered this shop. Harry was brought up in Britain but was sent home to look for a bride. With his new bride, he returned to Prestatyn in North Wales. They worked in their fish and chip shop in Prestatyn, where, Harry told us he also played football. When the family needed them to carry on the family business in

Cyprus they returned to Lefkara. Harry was a strong football fan and had some regalia on display to sell. In Lefkara, the women make the lace and the men make the filigree silver.

An old man in a nearby shop – you will have gathered by now that I like lace and Allen of course, being a metal man, likes the intricacies of working with metal – told me that he used to go to Lancashire. I said that I came from Leigh. It transpired, he said, that he used to go on Leigh Market to sell lace. I told him that my mother used to buy her mats & chair-back covers on Leigh Market. *Some years later, as you will soon read, we were able to take Mum to Cyprus and Lefkara. She met Harry and his wife and do you know? Harry remembered us.*

Larnaca.

While we still had the use of the car, we ventured out to Larnaca on the eastern end of the south coast. The promenade is tree-lined on one side. On the other is simply the beach filled with sunbeds which go down to the inviting coolness of the sea. Underneath the city is the ancient city of Kition. Legend has it that it [Kition] was established by one of Noah's grandsons in the thirteenth century BC. Who are we to argue?

At the top of the street that is home to the Church of Lazarus is a Fort with canons outside facing the sea. A plaque mentions 17-19AD. We explored inside among the many trees and walked along the walls finding the gardens a cool respite from the heat. This fort is a striking contrast to the modern building and Minaret [under scaffolding]. In contrast to this history a very modern aeroplane flew in over the sea to land at Larnaca Airport. I bet that if people in ancient times came back for a day they would think that they had come to another planet.

There was an archaeological site for the ancient ruins but I think it was closed at the times we were there and really; did *I* want to see more ruins? A better option was to walk around whereupon we discovered a Dolls House and a souvenir shop on a busy street. By the museum was a school. Down one street – and this made the day for 'his nibs' – what did we find?

'Allen found a workshop. You could come for a job.' [Engineer]He was always happy when he found a sheet metal workshop.

'You really are after a job, aren't you?'

We had come across stacks of pipes, box section, and all sorts and briefly ran through the possibilities.

'Yes.' The answer was uncompromising.

Driving home westwards, the setting sun was a golden ball in front of us turning the sky blood red on the horizon.

Would we come again?

The city of **Limassol** where we stayed on this visit sits on the seafront in between Larnaca and Pafos on the south of the island. Although very modern and cosmopolitan, Limassol has some preserved ancient monuments and ruins of its past. The main coast road is extremely busy but once across you can walk for miles along the seafront or rest on one of the many seats on this tree-lined promenade. Our hotel was comfortable and, being a studio apartment had the addition of a small table and two chairs, a settee and a kitchenette – which was not operational for our booked stay – and a breakfast bar. It all added to make our room more spacious.

There is so much to see on this wonderful island in the sunshine of the Mediterranean Sea; so much that we did not see on this, our first visit; so much that we would like to explore again.

Would we come again? Yes. And we did. Twice.

Return to Cyprus.

Some years after our visit to Cyprus and we fancied going there again and saw a good deal in the Over 50's holiday brochure for an 'all-inclusive' holiday with trips included. After talking to my husband, he agreed that, logistically, it was possible and I telephoned to see what the availability was. One bright morning, late in 2003 I dropped in unexpectedly on Mum (who was now on her own) and put my cards on the table so to speak.

'Is it set in stone that you won't fly?' I asked.

'Well . . ., she hedged. I quickly bit the bullet.

'There is a good deal here for a week in Cyprus. It won't be hot but will be better than here. Have a think but you will have to be quick as there are only a few places left.'

With that I left the ball in her court together with the brochure. Mum thought about flying and decided that yes, she would come to Cyprus with us in January 2004. I made all the arrangements such as adjoining rooms, airport assistance etc. and the all-important passport. Her first one.

Now Mum was a very good planner and at eighty-six years of age had lost none of her skills in this area. These included packing two weeks ahead of time and including all but the kitchen sink. She spent many happy hours deciding what clothes she would need and what she was going to put them in. As it was many years since she had travelled, her suitcases had seen better days and would not be secure enough for an aeroplane. Off we went to town where she informed me she had seen some nice trolley cases. With great restraint, I advised her on the best size bearing in mind the weight allowed explaining that if it was too big she would exceed her limit. The passport was next on the list; this involved a trip to the supermarket for a photo, plus lots of form filling.

One bright day, after I had re-packed her case efficiently whilst restraining her from packing her whole wardrobe, and with passport and Euros safely in her handbag, we set off for the airport. Mum could walk you understand, but the distances involved were great; we were also concerned about boarding and leaving the aircraft so I had organised wheelchair assistance. At check-in, we had to wait for this as a plane had arrived from Pakistan and most of the passengers wanted wheelchairs. Eventually one arrived and Airport Assistance staff wheeled Mum through to security and passport control.

Mum was well-wrapped up in trousers, warm fleece and her furry hat but was nonplussed at being asked to remove her hat so it could be checked to make sure she wasn't smuggling something through. For a lady of Mum's generation, being asked to remove her hat is like being asked to undress. We went for a cup of tea to recover. We needed this after all the checks at Security.

Very quickly, after the long delay in getting through security checks, we needed to make our way to the boarding gate and someone came to look for us as we were straggling. Airport assistance staff wheeled mum to the gate for boarding while we followed.

In the event, Mum was fascinated by the flight and all that went on with cabin service, toilets etc. but as we arrived in Cyprus it was wet and windy which made it impossible to bring out the lift for a wheelchair. Therefore, Mum had to struggle down the steps with her bag and walking stick to the tarmac and on to the terminal. With all passport procedures followed, we found the Saga bus and were taken to our hotel in

Limassol – a smaller one than we had stayed in previously but it was excellent.

Although listed as three-star hotel, the Kanika Pantheon or Kapetanios Odyssia, warranted four stars. Our host Henry Kelly was 'the host with the most' and made her feel very much at home on this her first overseas holiday ever. While waiting for the booking-in procedures to be completed and feeling rather jaded after the journey, Mum was glad of my offer to bring her a glass of whisky from the bar. Irish of course, but being imported, she had to pay. Not a problem. Just get the whisky.

Henry looked after everyone well, especially those who needed help. Mum was very impressed with the organization and the care which he showed her on this all-inclusive holiday. As requested when booking the holiday, Saga had arranged an adjoining room to ours, which was re-assuring for her and convenient for me to pop in to do her hair and help her as needed. The hotel was situated away from the main area of Limassol (which is very big), and had easy access to the sea front.

From here we caught the bus one day into the centre of Limassol where we did some shopping. At least I did as I needed a new pair of shoes but ended up with three pairs. Have I told you that I like shoes? I also bought a new purse/wallet. The shopkeeper was so desperate for the money to pay for a bus ride to visit his wife in hospital that he accepted a slightly lower price than advertised as I only had a ten Euro note with me. My money-keeper husband was no-where to be seen.

All in all, Mum loved the whole experience.

Along the coast and inland to Polis.

We hired a car to take her around the island. As driving is on the left and we had explored before, we knew where to go.

We had hoped to go into the Troodos Mountains to the Monastery but the extensive road works which were taking place rendered this inadvisable so we changed our plans, heading along the south coast towards Pafos and onwards to the northern coast. On our way to the north-west shore, we passed what is reputed to be Aphrodite's Birthplace. We stopped to stroll by the sea and took photos.

'There is Mum in front of Aphrodite's Rock. She is just deciding whether or not she should have a swim, which is what you are supposed to do.' I recorded with dry humour.

Mum meanwhile, helped by Allen as she negotiated the pebbles on the shore, had actually let go of that oh-so-heavy bag and rested it on a pallet of wood while she posed for the camera, fixing her warm fleece jacket in place. Apparently, this covered the shoulder bag around her neck. *Two bags?* Allen meanwhile was in shirt sleeves.

We never did find out what she carried in that shopping bag, but in later years we surmised that it was all her worldly goods including the 'loose' change that she collected. Probably all her money as well as I found some years later that she foolishly kept money in the house. Old habits die hard.

'It is a beautiful day today.'

I recorded what I could. Mum was calling to me but I couldn't catch it or rather, the camcorder couldn't. Huge lumps of rock stood out into the sea, which it was clear to see were Aphrodite's.

I continued to pan around the shore, 'on the south coast of Cyprus near Pafos', while the sea lapped quietly at the pebbly shore.

We continued on our way. Mum, in blue cardigan and headscarf had cast some of her 'skins' in the warm winter sunshine.

'We have stopped by Coral Bay beach and are just having our picnic lunch before we head a bit further north towards Polis.'

Mum, as happy as a sand boy as she sat on a bench overlooking the wide expanse of sea while she munched her sandwich, found it hard to take it all in and realize that she was in the middle of the Mediterranean Sea far away from home and close to places that she had read about in the Bible. Coral Bay is on the west of the island beyond Pafos and the Tombs of the Kings.

We were to stay here some years hence on another escape – literally – to the sun. We were so exhausted then with the hurly and burly of life and Allen not able to trek around as he did on this visit, or likes to, that we contented ourselves on that third visit with relaxing in our beach hotel.

Now, we were enjoying showing Mum the island. She sat quietly on a bench overlooking the sea – so far from a grey UK – with her thoughts as she absorbed the view, the sound of the sea, and her packed lunch. Amidst the tufts of grass by the roadside were clumps of large spiky cactus plants. It was a good road, bleached white in the strong Cypriot sunshine. Behind us was a large hotel and as with all the hotels on the coast around her, was very smart.

Lunch over, we were soon on our way. Allen covered the miles with ease, giving us glimpses of sea in the bay beyond as we turned inland and rose, with the Alcamas Peninsula on our left to the village of Polis ahead. We had re-joined the main road as it made for a smoother journey than driving on minor roads.

Coming again upon the village called Polis or Chrysochous [I explained Polis earlier], we found a simple but traditional bar high up above Chrysochou Bay. A sign on the wall told us that is was 'Brunnen Pub' whatever that meant. From the open front, tables and chairs of all kinds spilled out onto the terrace.

Inside the cooler interior were more tables and benches all painted in a lovely sea blue colour. Green plants tumbled from the roof and the supporting posts at the side. There was a national flag propped here and there amidst a basket of fruit and ashtrays. Looking carefully at the roof construction, Allen was fascinated. Mum simply sat quietly, drinking it all in. Behind her, a set of drums and cymbals shared space with a guitar, (maracas?), and a long instrument of some kind hanging from the wall.

Open windows and an open glass door led to the back of the building, or rather, inside the building. It looked as if a roof and two sides had been constructed to form an area for rest, drinking, music, and no doubt, dancing. Another wall was painted with brightly coloured shapes while more tables and chairs added to the confusion of this delightful find.

With sunshine flooding in through the open front of the building, we enjoyed a relaxing drink as we absorbed the views cascading down to the coast from our hilltop location.

Outside, a new building let customers know that they could find 'Toilets'. More tables, seats, and potted plants on the tiled terrace invitingly asked you to sit awhile and enjoy the wonderful view while birds cheeped away, supplying daytime music.

The owner of the bar was having a long conversation outside with an Irish man. Mum of course, was fascinated by this; to find an Irishman in this remote corner of this far away island. Eventually, the bar owner interrupted his conversation to come and serve us. Our drink was accompanied by plates of fruit and smiles from the owner. Mum enjoyed the Cyprus brandy so much that she asked if she could buy a bottle. The owner, found an empty vodka bottle, rinsed it out under the tap, and filled it from the cask before Mum put her treasure safely in her bag. I think that the alcohol content would have killed any lingering germs in the bottle – if they had time to be there long enough that is.

It was a long drive back from Polis to Limassol. Driving south through the hills via Stroumpi to Pafos we soon reached the motorway and our hotel passing Episkopi on the way.

Lefkara and lace-making.

One day, we went to Lefkara and Mum saw the lace being made. The video shows Mum, again all wrapped up in furry hat and fleece, sitting on a low stone wall in Lefkara with Allen. By her side was a bulging shopping bag – gripped tightly as if it might disappear. We joked that she had brought the kitchen sink (a saying in Lancashire that someone had brought all their belongings) it was so heavy. Allen thought that there were a couple of bricks in the bag.

Behind them on the low wall, tall evergreen Cypress trees rose into the winter sky, contrasting with bare deciduous trees and other evergreens of different shades.

'We are in Lefkara and have just had a cup of coffee and a brandy after lots of spending on my part. Rather Allen's part due to having bought my birthday present.'

(My birthday was in a few weeks' time in February and we had purchased a necklace and earrings in Harry's shop in Pano Lefkara or Upper Lefkara. I described this shop on our earlier visit.)

More on Lefkara at *http://virtualtourist.com*

Our film shows the modern front of a Bank. Beside it and in front of an embroidery/ lace shop sat a dark-haired lady who was busy with lace work. She looked very comfortable sitting on the wooden garden seat with wrought iron sides. On her lap rested a cushion on top of which lay an intricate piece of work. Cyprus embroidery is very unusual in that, if done properly you can't tell which is the 'right' side and which is the 'wrong' side where the tread is tied off. On a chair at her side lay a fluffy white dog with floppy ears and a black, button nose. The lady was Maria, Harry's wife.

Allen helped Mum to walk across in her sprightly way. At eighty-six years of age she couldn't half move but the bag weighed her down and the ground was uneven. Maria moved over to make room for Mum on the seat as Allen helped her to sit down. Still clutching her heavy bag by both handles, Mum hauled it on to her lap – she was noted for her strong grip as evidenced by the number of taps which she turned off so tightly that no-one else could turn them on again.

The lace making in Lefkara fascinated her. She eagerly examined the lace-making process and sat enthralled as she chatted to Maria who, as she stitched, explained all the stitches in the lace which she was making. This piece of lace looked like what we call drawn-thread work where threads (of one direction) are taken out and the threads left in the other direction are stitched together to form a pattern. This piece of work was an ecru/cream colour with the pattern formed with a pale brown thread. These skills are passed down through the generations – mother to daughter. Lefkara lace is exported worldwide.

LACE-MAKING IN LEFKARA.

Although many of the goods on display are handmade in Lefkara – embroidery, lace and silver goods worked by the men – there are of course, imported goods. In fact, the huge shop was very well stocked.

It was all so beautiful.

'We are going to make our way now to Larnaca,' I recorded. 'There is a castle there and the Church of Lazarus.'

Larnaca.

Arriving in Larnaca on the south-east coast after a smooth ride on a good road, we parked safely. Crossing the busy road, we reached the Church of Saint Lazarus. At this point, I was filming the ground as the camcorder, still switched on, swung by my side. *I am noted for leaving it switched on and you wouldn't believe how much footage of shoes tripping along a pavement we have.*

Allen and Mum entered the church from the covered, arched walkway. The walls of the church inside were of quite roughly hewn stone and brick. Much of this however, was decorated with richly carved, golden wall coverings behind the altar. This was roped off of course. Many candlesticks and candleabras cast a golden light among the gloom.

The church is in mainly Byzantine style dating from the ninth century. Some years ago, (1970) a crypt was discovered under the altar and the sarcophagus that was discovered, is said to be of Lazarus who – after he was raised from the dead by Jesus and ordained by Bishop Saint Barnabé – lived and worked in Cyprus as Bishop of Kition for thirty years. Looking at the map, it is clear how near to Bethany on the West Bank is Cyprus.

Kition is now known as Larnaca.

Bethany is now known as al-Eizariya at the foot of Mount of Olives west of Jerusalem.

Inside the church, richly carved light fittings and chests abounded. Stairs led down to the crypt. Allen went down to examine what was down there. The lighting was low but large golden lights hanging from the low roof cast a glow. I quickly filmed what I could but soon returned up to the main level.

Outside, a pair of pigeons, one black and white and one grey, were cooing and kissing, oblivious to all around. They were so sweet. It was strange to see such an ancient building with covered archways and cloisters situated so close to the noise and bustle of what is now a modern city.

We headed to the nearby large square campanile and spent some time looking out to sea.

After Larnaca, we drove to the coast where we stopped for a while and for a photo shoot.

'We are walking now by the Mediterranean Sea.'

I got a good shot of Mum posing for the camera and the noisy sea as it slapped into the shore in the background.

'I am not taking *you*,' I teasingly promised Allen as he turned to pose, nice and warm in his Gold Wing fleece.

'Which is the fort?' I queried. 'The old fort, isn't it?'

Allen was holding fast to Mum's arm to keep her safe from the traffic. The fort is of Turkish origin being built in the year sixteen hundred and twenty-five. It then became a prison but is now the Medieval Museum. Some of the artefacts from the ancient city of Kition are housed there.

Nicosia.

The holiday offered an included trip to Nicosia in the Turkish sector. Unfortunately, it poured down with rain. We visited a museum but as it was a wet day we could not stroll around as much as we would have liked to. We did however, have the experience of crossing into Turkish held Northern Cyprus after presenting our passports at Border Control [2004]. I feel that we left the coach before the border and walked across. We were only able to stroll a little way then and memory is unable to recall much apart from being very wet, cold, having to dodge puddles and find a cafe to have something to eat. I do remember that my red shoes cast a lot of red dye on my feet as they had sprung a leak. Photos and film were not allowed then so I have no record of our visit other than memory.

The holiday ended with a special dinner in the hotel which was so very comfortable with a very attentive host.

The flight home seemed much longer than the flight out to Cyprus. This Mum found quite tedious. Returning to the cold January skies of Manchester, we left Mum at home to unpack leisurely and sit with her thoughts as she re-lived her experiences – no doubt accompanied by a tot of Cyprus brandy from Polis.

******

In the summer of 2008 after another hectic year, we once again truly did 'escape to the sun' as I insisted on booking a last-minute relaxing holiday. Booking at the last minute is not our usual practice but this time it was a case of 'needs must'.

Being June, it was very hot. The modern hotel on the west coast was on the beach. Steps, roughly hewn into the rock led down from the sunbed area to the sands and the sea. Being north of Pafos, this modern hotel was not far from the Tomb of Kings but quite a way out of town and too far for us to walk. Did *I* really want to look at more archaeological sites? Well, no. Although there was a bus into town e were quite happy to simply relax, soak up the sunshine, and re-charge our batteries.

Would we return? Yes. Will we? Who knows. Perhaps one day. However, I am so thankful that when we could explore and walk the distances we grasped every opportunity with both hands and put more treasures into our box of memories.

~~~~~~

Atlantic
Adventure

MAP BY ANNIEBISSETT.COM
(NATIONAL GEOGRAPHIC EXPEDITIONS.COM)

The island of São Miguel. Azores.

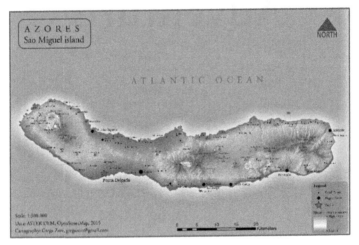

The Azores

The Portuguese islands of the Azores lie in the North Atlantic Ocean on a parallel line between Lisbon and New York, about one thousand three hundred kilometres west of mainland Portugal. They are volcanic islands and, lying in the path of the Gulf Stream, winters are generally mild. Of the nine islands that make up the archipelago, São Miguel to the east is the largest with the city of Ponta Delgada being the capital of the region. On the map, they appear to be dark and mysterious, very small blobs in the vast expanse of the North Atlantic Ocean and seemingly inaccessible all those years ago.

In our thirst for adventure and new horizons we realized, from the holiday brochure that wasn't ever far out of my reach, that it *was* possible to visit. Christmas of 1998 therefore, saw us in Ponta Delgada.

At that time, many people were looking to celebrate the turn of the century with something big. I worked out that if your first birthday is when you have completed twelve months of life or one year, then the year 2000 is the completion of two thousand years since Christ was born not the start. (Read on.) Therefore, by my convoluted reckoning the year 1999 was near enough to it being two thousand years since His actual birth. I realize that this may be disputed but it was near enough to have a celebration.

We also felt that everything would be very expensive at the turn of the century and when the Saga brochure – which we had recently started to receive – offered this trip to a distant island far into the darkness of the Atlantic Ocean, I was intrigued. The joint visit to Madeira, which we had visited before a few years previously, was a bonus; we had heard wonderful things about the firework display in Madeira when the old year gives way to the new.

This was our first time with Saga Holidays, a specialist over 50's holiday company. Being only in our early fifties at the time and at the younger end of the age group, we booked the trip with some trepidation; we were not sure if we were ready for this type of holiday with our perception of 'older people'. However, the company does organize some unusual holiday experiences. Deciding that we could always do our own thing as usual if we wanted to, we booked our places. It was certainly an experience to look forward to.

After driving to Gatwick Airport and leaving the car in a secure parking area nearby, the car parking company chauffeured us to the terminal building. That really was a bonus since we had not been to Gatwick Airport before. The queues were astounding; the sheer size of the airport overwhelming, so much so that we doubted if we would have found our own way if parking at the airport itself. Fortunately, our taxi driver could use the taxi lane whereupon he deposited us in good time at the correct arrivals entrance in the correct terminal. He explained that if we had been on our own and had stopped at all or parked up anywhere, our car would have been picked up and taken away. Not an encouraging thought.

The first leg of our journey was to Lisbon in Portugal where we had to disembark and quickly find the departure gate for the second leg of our journey from Lisbon to Ponta Delgada on the island of São Miguel. The excellent Air Portugal scheduled flight with lots of leg room made for a comfortable journey

There was only just enough time to disembark in Lisbon, find out where we had to go for the Ponta Delgada flight and race to the next boarding gate, and join the queue that was already boarding. With a sigh of relief that we hadn't missed the flight we were soon settled on a much smaller plane.

Locals who were returning for Christmas, carried all sorts of parcels from presents and computers to wrapping paper poking out of bags. In fact, everything but live chickens. It was mesmerizing.

Ponta Delgada at Christmas.

We flew in the setting sun to land at Ponta Delgada. I filmed the wing flaps opening as we came to land being entranced by everything – like a small child. A Saga representative met us at the airport which was re-assuring for us. The transfer by coach to our hotel in Ponta Delgada on the island of Sao Miguel was seamless with porterage of luggage taking the hassle out of everything. Our hotel had a lovely location with rooms and balconies overlooking the sea. They were well appointed, spacious and came with the special touch of fruit and bottled water in the room. This was welcome after a long journey.

The following morning, I filmed the seven o'clock sunrise over the bay. It was incredibly noisy with traffic and surprisingly warm. I could see cargo ships coming into harbour carrying everything loaded in containers, one with a tractor strapped on top.

At the Welcome Meeting, we were soon to find that **São Miguel** is a very beautiful & diverse island with lots to do and see.

One day, my husband went on a guided walk to the north of the island while I went to the hotel gym and then sunbathed on the roof of the hotel from where I could see the tower of the Church of San Pedro and the top of the market. The sea used to go up to where the square now is. They moved the gates of the city. From the roof, I could see a swimming pool and the bathing platform on the promenade. As we were in the Gulf Stream, the sea water was warm. In the harbour, I could see shipwrecks from earlier storms. Although we were experiencing lovely weather, three years earlier, at the same time of year, there had been very bad storms and ships were wrecked.

On his return to the hotel from his guided walk in the north of the island, my husband related to me how he saw dramatic coastlines and a farmer riding on a donkey collecting milk in milk churns in the fields, leaving dogs to guard the cattle. By contrast, the workday life in the south is more as we know it, with mobile phones in popular use in the city. He [my husband] surmised that the man on the donkey probably had a mobile phone in his pocket as well.

A FARMER IN THE AZORES 1998

Later that day we walked into the city to explore. From modern cars tooting their horns to three-wheeled trucks noisily revving their engines, from cobbled streets and smart shops found in the unspoilt square, to solid buildings at every turn, everything was a bustling, thrusting, thriving mixture of sights and sounds as cars, bikes and people vied for space.

The contrast was amazing. It was Christmas – locals rushed about in shirt sleeves in the warm air and yet, in the square, there stood Santa's Sleigh. An enormous display of lights like ribbons flowed from the centre of a maypole as the city prepared for Christmas which was only a few days away. Outside the fort, military guards paced up and down, swinging their swords. Overhead, the sky was blue. What a contrast.

Exploring the island.

We took advantage of the trips on offer, in order to see as much as possible of the island. We visited a **Pottery** where we all gathered around to watch the potter working the clay as she turned the wheel using various tools to achieve the shape she demanded. It was not high tech. The patterns were mainly country style patterns in blue and white but there was some fine china being worked on and on display. We were allowed to watch the painters as they brought the flowers sketched on the articles to life.

Continuing our tour, our next stop was a visit to a **Blacksmith**. Now this was an eye-opener and a step back in time. The poor horse was led into position. The blacksmith held its hoof between his legs as a litter of puppies nestling nearby shouted either their noisy encouragement, or simply protestations at being ignored. The blacksmith moved an old plough out of the way. It really *was* ancient and a real museum piece but no doubt in good working order. The blacksmith then roped up the horse's leg against a post so that he would not get kicked by the horse as he put a shoe on the back foot. It was astonishing that that kind of place still existed.

Leaving the blacksmith and boarding the coach we turned northwards towards the coast. It was cooler and very windy with glimpses of fishermen in little boats. A church with one hundred and four steps up to the top – all in planned stages with walls to separate the sections – was home to a little shrine in the small chapel of **Lenda da Senhora de Paz**. From its high vantage position above the island we drank in the fantastic views down to the sea. As usual there was a shop here tourists could buy souvenirs. All around, waving in the wind were groups of red hot pokers flowering in abundance.

Along the coast, we wandered to a little harbour in a village where a group of small, barefooted boys, fascinated by the camcorder, vied to have 'their' face in the frame. They appeared to be very poor but happy as they shouted noisily.

In the south, we saw another church all square towers and squat in what used to be the capital – **Villa Franca do Campo**. On the way to the lakes in the west, we stopped in the gardens of the **Presidential Residence** where my husband tapped the trees like Woody Woodpecker. Our guide explained that the President did not live there as his wife was satisfied with her current house. The previous President was not married and lived at home with his mother.

LENDA DA SENHORA DE PAZ.

Reaching the lakes – **Caldeira das Sete Cidades** – the sun was going down so we did not get the full effect of what the lakes were famous for and had hoped and come to see. When the sun shines on the water, one appears blue and one appears green. These lakes are very dramatic and are accessible by bus. In the crater is the village of Sete Cidades.

CALDEIRA DAS SETE CIDADES

Christmas was in full swing and, that evening, we strolled around the streets. Beautiful lights were strung from building to building and around archways and windows. Jolly music was playing Christmas Carols; the trees in the square were lit up. After a (for us) late start to decorating the town and the shops, the display was well worth the wait and it fully captured the true spirit of Christmas.

I was particularly entranced by the dancing Santa's in the shops. They were fun and at the first opportunity at home, I bought one to entertain our grandchildren. Eventually the grown-ups got tired of *Jingle Bell Rock* and it had to be switched off.

To the north of São Miguel.

With two days to go before Christmas Day, morning broke with a plane coming in over the sea to land in the nearby airport. The sunrise shot orange lights across the water. Today we were going on a trip to the north. There was so much to see on this small island and as we might never come again, intended to make the most of every opportunity presented to absorb the feel and culture of the island. It was only small but packed with many delights.

The north of the island was windy. The sea crashed against the rocks on this dramatic coastline. At the **Whaling Station,** my husband examined the winch. This was steam driven and was still in use to pull whales in from the sea. There were many fishing boats littering the shore.

Our tour took us to **Ribeira Grande** and the **Hydro Station**. The guide was very informative; Allen lapped it all up. Using the remote control on the camcorder, we could have a rare shot of us together by setting up the camcorder on a wall and setting the delay timer.

Leaving the north, to make our way to the **Lago de Fogo** or **Fire Lake** – there was a good view of the coast from the highway. We found that the Lago de Fogo was in the middle of a crater and almost the highest mountain in the Azores. The beautiful views rounded off another exciting day.

LAGO DE FOGO

Swimming on Christmas Eve and more . . .

Christmas Eve dawned with yet another dramatic sunrise over the sea. In the distance, we could see a big boat moored off shore. Following our guide and boarding our coach, we headed for **Santana** on the north-east of the island. She explained that here, the people have blue eyes and brown hair.

(Watching the video later, Allen explained that as the road meandered down we ended up looking backwards. The fields were divided by bamboo and had taken over the road.)

On the north coast, we went to the only tea plantation in Europe. Allen was fascinated and thrilled to look at the machines one of which came from Manchester which is only a few miles from where we grew up. In fact, the machine was made at the firm where his brother worked. Inside, we were given a demonstration of how the tea leaves were sorted. Outside, a cow grazed quietly. Was its milk for the tea?

Heading now to the **Furnas Valley** we all gathered round to watch men from a nearby hotel prepare our lunch. Huge vats of the typical dish of meat and vegetables (cabbage) were placed carefully in cooking holes in the ground where the heat of the earth and the steam would cook our meal for us. With the crater being near to the centre of the earth the water in the hole boiled away furiously, cooking the meal. The whole crater was covered in bubbling holes with explosions of steam. It was astounding.

Leaving our lunch to cook, our guide took us to the **Botanical Gardens** next door to the beautiful hotel where we would lunch. Being forewarned, I and others had packed a swimsuit. Along with a few other guests, after changing in the changing huts in the gardens, I swam in the therapeutic, naturally hot, outdoor pool that was set among all kinds of plants and trees. The huge circular pool was very old; unlike modern-day swimming pools it was built with brick with a huge spout dispensing the warm therapeutic water from its source into the pool. This surprising experience, added to the lovely warm day in this remote part of the island, lent an air of unreality to what was Christmas Eve.

Returning to the crater and standing at a safe distance, we watched as the men used long poles with hooks to fish out the pot from the hot ground. This pot was covered in cloth – rather as our Christmas Puddings are when steamed – and contained our lunch, all nicely cooked in this crater near to the centre of the earth. The men carefully placed this pot in a van to take back to the hotel kitchen. You wouldn't really believe that you could cook your lunch in the ground until you had witnessed it. It was hard to envisage.

A family of ducks followed us back to the coach which would take us along the lake back to the hotel for lunch before going to the hot springs. Perhaps the ducks wanted to share our meal.

It was very hot by now [after lunch] and were glad of cool clothes. The **Central Thermas of Furnas** are pools of boiling water which come from the earth's core. Stand well back as they explode without warning with jets of boiling water shooting up into the air. All the pools had a name. A nativity scene with lambs and shepherds had been set among the rocks and landscape. It was like a miniature village.

As we passed through **Villa Franca** on the way back to the hotel we reflected on another beautiful day which would end with a special Christmas Dinner in our hotel before we attended Midnight Mass at the church around the corner.

PRETTY FURNAS LAKE IN THE FURNAS VALLEY

Christmas Day in Ponta Delgada.

Christmas Day was surprisingly very hot. I stood on our balcony and watched as a bright orange sun broke through the darkness of night, shooting beams of light onto the slumbering sea. A few locals took an early morning dip from the bathing platform or sailed their boats. After lunch, we strolled along the promenade in the warm sunshine stopping for a photo shoot where an obliging fellow guest took a picture as we snuggled together on the sea wall in summer clothes.

Our holiday Rep. on the island had looked after us like a mother hen, even leaving her family on Christmas Day to join us for Christmas Dinner. In Portugal, they celebrate Christmas in a different way to us and didn't have a large meal in the middle of the day but saved it for evening. As well as the hotel giving us a little present of an embroidered neck cover for a wine bottle (the embroidery was the traditional blue), our Rep. gave us each a rectangular-shaped paper weight made of grey volcanic stone topped with a brass whale-shaped object. I still use it and am looking at it as I type.

What a wonderful Christmas.

Tomorrow we would leave this lovely island of contrasts and fly to Madeira to welcome in the New Year and see the spectacle of the fireworks over Funchal.

~~~~~~

Madeira

The transfer from Ponta Delgada to Funchal was uneventful. We already knew from an earlier visit that Funchal airport had a short, very short, runway due to the land rising steeply from the sea. It was so short that on approaching from the sea the pilot would appear to be heading into sheer rock. Consequently, you felt that the aeroplane was going to crash into the rock face.

However, the skill of the pilot as he slammed on his brakes at the last minute saved us from destruction as he completed a safe landing. *We later found on yet another visit that the airport had been extended to incorporate a longer runway. It was such a relief.*

The highlight and purpose of **this** return visit to Madeira after our stay in the Azores was to be the New Year Eve's firework display in the hills over the bay of Funchal where the Saga Ruby cruise ship and other cruise ships call in to hoot their horns to welcome in the New Year.

Funchal in Madeira was a lovely as ever.

On our first visit, we had stayed at a hotel linked to the Hotel Savoy, where we dined each night. Oh yes. We have been spoiled. As a first experience of Madeira, it was second to none and we were lucky enough to have ringside seats at the Miss Portugal Competition as we dined. (More on that later.)

This time, we stayed a little further out and up a slight hill at the Quinta do Sol. Set in lovely gardens, this hotel had the advantage of a roof-top terrace from where we were to watch the fireworks on New Year's Eve. Meanwhile, we set out to enjoy our stay and the gentle stroll into Funchal centre in the winter sunshine.

Exploring in and around Funchal.

Having taken advantage of all the excursions on our last visit, we now spent some time exploring farther afield on foot and by bus. Deciding that we wanted to re-visit the village of Monte in the hills high above Funchal, Allen bravely said that he would suffer the bus as I was not about to **walk** all that way uphill. Walk? Well I would walk down but certainly not up.

The journey by road was a tortuous experience as the driver flung the bus around the bends with much crashing of gears. It would be good on a Gold Wing motorbike we thought but for now, we had to make do. As we reached Monte in the hot sun we soon found some cool shade in the square.

Dressed in typical Madeiran costume of a black waistcoat over his white shirt and a pointy hat, and old, blind man sitting under the trees was happily playing his accordion. The gentle but lively music added another dimension to the tranquil setting as we gazed among the trees down the hill to Funchal and beyond.

A tradition in Monte is to have a ride in the baskets down the hill. As we had done this last time (and were still catching our breath) we decided to watch as the tobogganers who were dressed in white, some with red sashes and straw boaters, set couples into the baskets for the journey down the hill. The two tobogganers pushed off using their feet as brakes as the basket gathered speed on the hair-raising ride down to Funchal.

Strolling around Monte we went into the church which had a lovely crib (Nativity scene). As we later wended our way down the hill, on foot I may add, the views were ever-changing; you could see all over Funchal and the new motorways which had been built.

(On our later unexpected 3rd trip, we went up to Monte in the new Cable Car – it was much better.)

Now, continuing to stroll down the steep road we stopped to watch babbling streams as they poured out from under the road into a waterfall, rushing to tumble over the rocks below as they continued their hasty journey to the sea.

Reaching Funchal, we noticed that it was now very busy. There we saw what appeared to be a large collection of walking balloons. The man holding them was hidden under his display. A street artist was doing charcoal drawings from photos. In the centre of the city was a life-sized Nativity arrangement with all the figures clothed in beautiful costumes.

Cars, bikes, buses, and music all combined to give Funchal at Christmas it's unique flavour. On the central reservation along the main street were displays of Madeiran life while mothers dressed in traditional costume played with their babies. Other displays showed various aspects of traditional crafts. All this was set to a background of the abundant flora and fauna of Madeira.

My husband was keen to explore further afield. To this end, one morning we set out, armed with our umbrellas, to walk above Funchal to San Antonio, Nazaré and back. Although it had rained at seven o'clock, by ten o'clock the sun was shining making our umbrellas redundant while making for a pleasant walk.

In the afternoon, we walked through the hotel gardens and through the woodland into a cutting under the road bridge. In the stillness, water rushed down through the gully into the sea as we made our way back up from the other side of the road ready for another Saga dinner. As it was New Year, the hotel was also putting on special dinners and cocktail parties so we were well catered for.

When darkness fell, the lights came on in the streets, Funchal donned its evening clothes in the shape of fantastic decorations and evening bustle, while on the bridge, there was a fantastic curtain of light on either side of the road.

Night-time tour of Funchal.

One evening, we were taken in a mini-bus on a trip around Funchal to see the lights in the villages above the city. Our driver then drove down to the harbour where the New Year's disco was being set up ready for the festivities before cruising through the lighted streets of Funchal to see all the displays. This was fairyland personified and unforgettable. As usual, some people could not wait to set off their fireworks and we heard a few whistles and bangs as they got some practice in.

The motorway bridge was clearly visible in the distance as it wended its way around the hills and across the valley. We had a clear view of the lights shining down we could also see, as we drove on, the Casino and the harbour. This part of the journey retraced our steps of our earlier walk.

The driver, recounting local customs, explained to us that there were nine days of praying before Christmas and then people went to church, starting early in the morning, ringing bells, and waking everyone up. They prepare a chicken soup for a meal after Midnight Mass and carry on until three o'clock the following morning. Then, they have a turkey dinner on Christmas Day in the afternoon. (Well, I suppose they must sleep some time.)

Down in the city, the harbour area was set up for New Year festivities while ships visit to see the fireworks over Funchal. The lights in the city were amazing with every available surface appearing to be lit, while the designs were varied and well worth the trip. This display, on a small island in the Atlantic, puts into shade anything seen in the UK.

Fireworks over Funchal.

The fireworks on New Year's Eve were out of this world. The best view on the island was from the rooftop terrace of our hotel, the Quinta del Sol where we all gathered later in the evening. Some early fireworks went off in the distant hills – one was from part way up an apartment block.

I then had a total surprise as I had always thought that the fireworks were in the harbour area. In fact –all the villages in the hills above Funchal had set up synchronised fireworks. As these synchronised displays exploded in a blaze of colour and fire in the hills above Funchal at midnight, the brightly decorated cruise ships in the harbour sounded their horns in a wonderful noisy, medley of sound. The sound of car horns added to the noisy confusion as they were pressed to greet the New Year; more and more 'gunshot' sounds rent the air as fireworks exploded in bursts of colour, raining down to light the inky darkness of the sky. It was relentless.

The planned and co-ordinated display, exploding in the air for miles around as gunpowder, released from the confines of their containers in the ground below, sent bursts of colour again and again into the darkness of the night sky. It went on and on, appearing to be never-ending. It was truly wonderful and indescribable as eventually, momentum reached a climax. Ships in the harbour eventually sounded their appreciation and farewells before sailing away, while from our vantage point on the rooftop terrace of the hotel we joined other guests to welcome in 1999 with a glass of Champagne.

******

A floating garden in the ocean.

Our first visit however, to this 'floating garden' in the warm waters of the Atlantic Ocean had been a few years previously. It was in 1991 to be exact. Receiving some compensation for a car accident when I had been treated to a 'rear end shunt whilst stationary' we decided to splash out and start to expand our horizons. We had gone then, in the late Spring when the temperatures were high and the air humid.

After disembarking at the airport and clearing customs we found our holiday Rep. waiting to greet us. On the journey from the airport to our hotel, she warned us that,

'Even if it is cloudy, you need to cover up. Remember that we have an African sun and the sun's rays penetrate the clouds. You can still burn.'

Our hotel on this first visit was just outside the centre of Funchal and in the grounds of what was then the very plush Hotel Savoy with gardens that ran down to the sea.

(On our last and 3rd visit we found that a brand-new hotel had been built in the lower gardens named the Royal Savoy.)

Now however, we were to stay in the Hotel Santa Isabel in the same grounds which offered bed and breakfast accommodation with dinner being enjoyed in the restaurant of the Hotel Savoy itself. The best of both worlds we thought. Keeping within budget but with a taste of luxury.

The lush and shady gardens spread out from the immediate grounds of the hotel, across a small narrow road from where the view down to the sea was picture postcard perfect, into another garden which led down to the pool area (where I almost drowned one day).

I often paused in this secluded garden with its winding paths and exotic trees such as kapok to drink in the peace and solitude, looking up through the trees at the clear blue sky at what I thought was paradise. At this point in my life I was in stunned awe of the beauty around me. Never had I thought that one day this distant dream of mine, to visit this floating garden in the Atlantic, would become a reality. Nor was I to know that we would re-visit twice more in the future.

One day as we relaxed by the pool I decided to cool off with a quick dip in the inviting water. Not being a confident swimmer, I carefully negotiated my way into the shallow end and inched round to find where the pool went deeper. Satisfied, I ventured away from the edge when all at once, whoosh, the bottom of the pool where I was standing fell away and was no more. It wasn't built with a gradual slope but a shelf with an abrupt drop.

Well, I went under. Allen, with his nose in a magazine as he lazed on a sunbed some distance away, was oblivious to my cries for help. Fortunately, a passing hotel guest saw my difficulties and jumped in to save me before I drowned. Thanking him effusively, I tottered back to our sunbeds and my oblivious husband who was engrossed in a magazine; no doubt a motorbike or car magazine. Allen looked up in surprise.

'I could have drowned.'

I was indignant that he would have been minus a wife and none the wiser, Of course, he was now all sympathy and apologies but I knew to keep nearer to the edge in future.

From our sunbeds overlooking the sea, we could see the ocean divers at the long man-made jetty below us. Allen liked to walk along there, no doubt looking for crabs.

The narrow road between the gardens and the hotel led onto the main road but there was also a little road off which took you to a small church and a dead end. The tiny church was very ornate and richly decorated, perched as it was on the edge of a cliff with railings protecting you from a sheer drop down to the sparkling sea below. We loved to go there on a Sunday morning.

Heading from the hotel along the narrow road the other way, we liked to stop and admire the flowers in the flower shop. We had never seen the Bird of Paradise (Strelizias) or Protea flowers. (Now of course, our local flower shops and supermarkets can obtain these easily.) Entranced as we were by these exotic flowers we arranged to have some delivered to our hotel just before we were due to return home. The airline was quite used to stowing boxes of flowers in the hold of the aeroplane.

Wandering at will in Funchal.

We loved to wander from the hotel in the early morning along the main road into town, admiring the shops, the views, the long curve of the Casino Park Hotel and Casino overlooking the harbour and Santa Caterina gardens, and as we came to the centre of this wonderful old capital of Madeira's city centre, the variety of yachts, boats, cruise liners and naval ships in the harbour.

Surprisingly, the street signs were in both Portuguese and English, a testament to years gone by when there was a large English influence with soldiers garrisoned here.

The colourful market is famous. Local ladies dress in the typical Madeiran costume of red skirt with colourful stripes from waist to hem, waistcoat, white blouse, and a pointed black hat.

In the market, the choice and size of fish seemed never-ending. One fish looked *very* unappetising. It was scabbard fish; the one that we had been advised to try before we saw it in the market as it its appearance belied its delicious taste; we would have been put of this delicate morsel if we saw it first as it came out of the sea before eating it.

The abundant displays of fruit and enormous vegetables in wicker baskets, the masses of flowers and the cries of stall holders shouting their wares all added to this unique atmosphere.

In the harbour, we were treated to the sight of a boat being built. Passing the many gardens with their tumbling profusion of lush vegetation and exotic flowering plants, the water playing from the cool fountains invited you to sit awhile and rest to enjoy the beauty around you. The old town is full of culture and history.

Overlooking the harbour is fort of St Laurence or São Lourenço where, in a niche above a gate, is a statue of the saint who lived in the early years of the first century. The building was impressive with white walls offset by brown-framed windows. The many street cafes and tree-lined streets all added to the atmosphere. We wandered in the Rua de Santa Maria, the oldest street in Funchal dating back to the fourteenth century.

In contrast, when my husband stopped at a very modern car he was intrigued to see that it was fitted out with two steering wheels. One for the learner driver and one for the driving instructor. We had never seen that before. Two sets of pedals, yes, but not two steering wheels.

Over to the east of Funchal at the far end of the waterfront is the Fortaleza of São Tiago or Fort of Saint James. This mustard yellow building sits right by the sea ready to defend the city. We were only able to see from the outside as a soldier was standing in his sentry box forbidding entry. The sentry box was brightly decorated in red and gold stripes with a little canopy above to keep the guard cool from the hot sun.

Our mission that morning was to visit the famous Garton Greenhouses or Boa Vista Orchids. Situated just outside the city centre, the **Quinta do Boa Vista** houses the famous Garton Greenhouses where you will find the most exotic orchids which have been cultivated over many years. The Boa Vista Orchid Garden was founded by the late Group Captain Cecil Garton in the late 1960's. Many other beautiful flowers apart from orchids are cultivated there. Madeira is not called a 'floating garden' for nothing. The climate lends itself to an abundance of vegetation and the cultivation of exotic plants. It is kept green by the many rivers and their tributaries which flow down from the mountains in the centre of the island.

A strike and a beauty contest.

We had some wonderful dining experiences at the Savoy Hotel, not least due to a strike of waiters. Staff were not allowed to serve us but to ensure that their level of service did not drop, they had prepared and arranged a buffet meal. This was sumptuous with all manner of delectable dishes accompanied by our choice of wines.

Another evening was the occasion of the Miss Portugal Beauty Contest. As we were booked in to dine each evening, we were a little concerned when we saw that the restaurant was being transformed with a stage area for contestants and reserved tables for dignitaries and other notable people. The head waiter assured us that we would still have our table. He did not disappoint. We had a ringside seat right on the edge of the stage. Each table was decorated with a selection of tasty treats with a moulded chocolate bathing contestant in the middle.

With entertainment provided by the music of Paquette and Tony Cruz, resident musicians of the Savoy Nightclub Group, the occasion opened with a parade of contestants in variations of the national dress. After more songs by Tony Cruz, the girls had changed into cocktail dresses for another parade up and down the stage. The judges were the Secretary-General of the Tourist Board, the Head of Radio, the former winner and others. One photo shows myself and Allen in the background so I think that our nice head waiter must have obliged and taken a photo with our camera.

A display of leisurewear followed before the main part of the evening got underway. Allen had a bird's eye view of proceedings as the contestants paraded up and down on the raised stage a few feet away. All in all, there were fourteen girls; in truth, most were winners of one title or another. My photographs show that there was the winner of a minor title followed by the winner of another minor title and yet again another minor title. One of these also won the Miss Funchal title and went on to win third place in the Miss Madeira contest before second place was announced and finally the winner of Miss Madeira was crowned. I think the money prize was something like $1,000,000 Escudos. Last year's winner crowned this year's winner as is usual.

The number of photographs is unbelievable as Allen clicked away, especially the ones where the girls paraded in skimpy bathing costumes – when they turned their backs to us to congratulate the winner, I think that he got a little hot under the collar then. He certainly had an eyeful. Our ringside seat really *was* very close to the catwalk.

The following day, we were in a café near the hotel where the contest was being shown on TV. And there was himself right in the middle of the screen.

The Monte experience.

A visit to Funchal is not complete without a visit to the small village of Monte in the hills above Funchal. (I think that we must have gone up there as part of an excursion.)

As I explained earlier on our second visit, this is famous for the ride down the mountainside in a specially designed basket. Riding down the mountainside sounds simple but is an experience not to be missed or, underestimated as the baskets gather speed while the drivers steer around the corners down, down, through the village into the outskirts of Funchal. Certainly, the ride down was an experience never to be forgotten.

After wandering around the village and the cool, shady square, we took our place in one of the two-seater wicker sledges. The ride down to Funchal was fast and furious as the traditionally dressed men in their white clothes, and straw hats pushed us off, steering and braking with their rubber-soled boots while the toboggan gathered speed as it raced through the narrow streets with high walls at either side of the road, (just missing an old man on a corner who was struggling up the hill while leaning heavily on his walking stick); only just avoiding a crash into the frequent blind corners as we hung on for dear life on the two kilometre trip downhill. What an exhilarating ten minutes.

Of course, as is the case the world over, a selling opportunity is not to be missed and, at the appropriate point, the baskets are halted for a photo opportunity. With the wonders of modern technology, on this first visit a man had set up with a digital camera and by the time that the baskets and their cargo reached the end of the journey, the photo has been sent down the line to a computer at the bottom and printed out, ready for an instant sale as a memento of the trip.

THE MONTE EXPERIENCE – DOWN TO FUNCHAL ON THE COAST

Visiting the wine lodges.

No visit to Madeira is complete without a visit to one or two of the wine lodges. Our meanderings into the centre of Funchal brought us to the flower-decked entrance of the Madeira Wine Company Ltd. which housed a fine selection of Madeira wines. In the UK, we often think that Madeira wine is simply that – a wine – but it is far more complex than we first imagine.

Madeira wine is a fortified Portuguese wine and as with sherry, Madeira wine comes in a variety of styles ranging from dry to sweet. The Sercial, Verdelho, Bual, and Malmsey are the main grape varientals used. Once inside the wine lodge, you are usually able to see a selection of very old wines kept behind glass cabinets for security. At the end of a short tour, it is pleasant to sit down and try the different varieties.

The São Francisco Wine Lodges on the Avenida Arriaga near the Municipal gardens are another experience. The wine lodge has its own chapel as it was originally a 16th century Franciscan Monastery. They offered a guided tour, taking you through two centuries of what they call 'living wine history'. Not only did we see the great barrels where the wine is stored as it matures we were treated to a demonstration of how the barrels were built and formed. This information, alone was an education that all added to the experience. The museum houses ancient letters, documents, and tools which used to be used. It is clear to see how things have progressed.

On display in glass-fronted cabinets were huge bunches of different varieties of grapes. Further on, were examples of old wine presses and a goat (or sheep) skin which in days gone by were used to keep wine. At the end of the tour there was the usual wine tasting experience. Some vintage wines were on display and available for tasting, at a price. I have the original price list which of course is in the old currency of Portuguese Escudos. It shows that in 1991, a 1934 glass of Cossart Gordon Verdelho (medium dry) was priced at 900$00 Escudos or £3.75 GBP. It had been matured in an oak cask for fifty-two years before being bottled in 1986. I really savoured the smell, the taste. At £3.75 (twenty-five years ago,) it was worth savouring.

I have a photo of me holding a bottle of an 1882 Cossart Gordon Verdelho priced (1991) at 38.500$00 Escudos or £144 GBP. I was careful not to drop it.

There were of course, many other smaller wine lodges. In fact, I remember that we passed one on a stroll from our hotel towards the Lido to the west.

A visit to lace a factory.

Madeiran lace is famous and to be sure that you have the genuine article it is essential that you only buy goods with a little silver blob sewn into the edge to guarantee authenticity.

On our way to the lace factory, the excursion took us to the **Botanical Gardens** from where there were fine views down to the harbour, the **Quinta** which used to belong to the **Blandy** family – famous for their Madeira wines – a leather shop, and the Wicker Work Centre in **Camancha**.

The afternoon ended with what all the ladies were waiting for – a visit to the **Lace Factory** in the centre of Funchal. The factory allowed us to see all aspects of production; the design, printing of the design onto fabric ready for embroidery, laundry and pressing. One lady had a few scraps of material in her pocket which she slid over to us in return for a few coins. As the genuine Madeiran lace is so expensive, an affordable present is a handkerchief which has a little lace on a corner. But make sure that is has the seal of authenticity. The little blob of silver sewn into the edge.

An 'Espetada' evening.

The Espetada is a typical Portuguese dish. Large chunks of beef that have been rubbed in garlic and salt are skewered onto large stick before being cooked over hot coals. This of course, means that you are eating from the stick or at least, serving yourself from the stick. Wines and lively folk music by Trio Atlántico accompanied the meal at the Restaurante Típico A Seta, to which we were taken by coach along with other clients of the hotel. It was hilarious as we found ourselves sampling this new way of eating.

Island tour.

I have related many of our experiences on our first visit in 1991 to this wonderful island in the North Atlantic Ocean. This first visit was a visit that we had never envisaged that we would be able to make and, not knowing that we *would* be able to come again, wanted to absorb as much about the island that we could. Booking on a full day trip of the island was a 'must do' for us. We were not disappointed.

Our tour guide explained to us that he had had to study for three years to become an official guide. We were therefore assured of an informative day. He explained that no more building of hotels was allowed in the centre of Funchal. All newer buildings were spread further out. This was to preserve the culture and not spoil it by making it 'touristy'. Indeed, on later visits we observed how hotels were built further and further out and older buildings were undergoing renovation.

Leaving Funchal and heading through the village of **Camara de Lobos** into the mountains, our first stop was at **Cabo Girão**. This is the second highest cliff in the world with spectacular views. You don't want to get too close to the edge or you might feel a little dizzy when you see the drop down the sheer cliff face. After taking photographs from all angles, we headed back to the coach to continue along the coast to **Ribeira Brava**, a charming village by the sea where it was interesting to wander around to get a flavour of life outside the bustle of Funchal.

Popping into the church which was decorated with exotic floral displays, I was captivated by the difference in floral display arrangements in other parts of the world. One display had red and orange carnations seemingly coming out of a piece of driftwood. Another had a mass of what I came to know as anthuriums. Growing at the end of a tall stem, these have a waxy heart-shape with a central 'spike' growing out of the middle. The colours were a deep, rich red or orange offset by deep green foliage. At the time, these were unheard of where we lived in Wales but now, as with protea and strelitzias, they are more readily available, even in the supermarkets.

Our journey now took us into the interior of the island; into the **National Park** and the **Paul da Serra** plateau. In contrast to the warmth and sunshine of the coast, up here it was chilly; the light jackets that we had brought with us were very welcome. Standing as if on top of the world, we absorbed the wonderful views one of which was a levada channel. The levada channels that take water to various parts of the island are a feature of Madeira. The dramatic folds in the mountains were not like anything that we had seen before.

Now on the western side of the island from our vantage point in the Paul da Serra it was marvellous journey through the mountains to **Porto Moniz** on the north-west coast. The roads twisted and turned in a spaghetti-like way as we headed down out of the mountains to the coast. In the rocky shore, nature has created natural swimming pools which are replenished with fresh seawater when the tide rises. There is a lighthouse here at the end of the rocks to warn sailors of impending danger. Looking back to the mountain, you can see the many terraces flowing down the mountainside in tiers that have been dug out to give a flat growing area to cultivate produce.

Our tour continued along the northern coast, passing through many villages as we went. Due to the formation of the land, many twists and turns took us inland again before we had a brief stop at **Arco de São Jorge**. Geographically, São Jorge is in a line with Funchal on the other side of the island over the mountains. It lies in the far north of the island. The difficult journey is rewarded with spectacular views of the rugged mountains and sea. At one point, we could see a waterfall flowing out of the mountain down the sheer cliff into the sea. Not far away is the village of **Santana**.

Santana is well known for the traditional 'pointy' houses. These are of triangular construction, the straw roofs coming from a tall ridge at the top and sloping down almost to the ground at each side. The walls are white with red doors and window shutters. Some have a blue trim. They are so charming and it is wonderful to see how they have been preserved as an example of life on the island as it used to be. Our tour ended here as we headed back to our hotel.

Last night of our first visit to Madeira.

After dinner at the end of our visit, the hotel provided us with a Portuguese evening experience. Male dancers in white shirts, baggy trousers and little short boots danced energetically with their lady partners who were dressed in the traditional, colourful red-striped Madeiran costume. At the end, everyone was invited to join in which most of the guests did, holding hands as they danced around in a circle with much clapping of hands at various points.

It was time to say good-bye. As far as we were concerned then, it was a once-in-a-lifetime experience. We were not to know that a few years later I would stick more pins in a map when I saw the Saga Holidays brochure and set off once again into the Atlantic Ocean to spend Christmas in the Azores and New Year in Madeira – as I related at the start of this section in our story.

Even then, we thought that twice was a bonus. However, a few more years after that second visit, and needing to escape again from the responsibilities crowding in on us, I realized that we had several Air Miles that we needed to use up. To see the New Year in again in Madeira would be exciting.

Off I went with head buried in travel brochures. Or rather, with the Internet being so popular I trawled around it, booked a flight, found a hotel for a few nights, and off we set.

******

Hotel Lido for New Year.

By now it was the year 2002 with a promise of a new dawn in 2003. We found that our room was on the ground floor of the hotel with doors out onto a terrace. A manager (owner?) appeared to be working in the room next door and I still wonder if he had given up his room. As we had booked room only we had bought supplies of food for breakfast which I romantically enjoyed on our private terrace, although on leaving we found that our tariff had included breakfast but never mind; I enjoyed a leisurely breakfast on the private terrace surrounded by exotic plants and greenery.

The hotel was a little out of the centre of Funchal but the longer walk wasn't a problem for either of us then. Retracing our steps to places previously visited, we discovered that the Hotel Savoy had changed. The Santa Isabel building was still there but we never found out what is was used for. The Hotel Royal Savoy had been built in the lower gardens and nearer to the sea.

Visiting the Quinta do Sol hotel of our second visit we decided to venture further and walk along the dried-up river bed. Being near to the Lido, we had to walk past the famous Reid's Hotel to get into the city. Buses were frequent and sometimes welcome. It was a long slow uphill walk. On the way, we noticed that many elegant seemingly neglected and derelict properties were undergoing a major refurbishment programme to restore them to their former glory.

One day, the weather being overcast, we decided to venture out a bit further into the countryside and headed out. We just followed a signpost and a map. Coming to one inhabited area, we also found that we were near what seemed to be a military camp with soldiers carrying guns. I think that we were looking for a levada as the guide books say that you should walk along one if you want to see the true country. However, we didn't really do that but just enjoyed the experience of exploring before the rain came down and finding our way back to the coast.

More fireworks.

On New Year's Eve, the hotel management laid on coaches to take hotel clients to the **Football Stadium** to watch the firework display. Before we climbed into the coach, a waiter handed each of us a plastic champagne flute. Bemused, we took it. After all we didn't have any champagne with us. We soon found out what that was for. At the stadium, we all filed into our seats, relishing the balmy night air. All at once, a bottle of champagne was handed down the row for us to fill our glasses. Surprise, surprise, it was the policeman handing out the bottles as he joined in with the relaxed occasion while at the same time keeping order.

Again, near to midnight the fireworks started to go off, synchronised as they were in the hills of the villages strung out above Funchal. Again, they were awe-inspiring, breath-taking, colourful and a work of art. The explosions went on and on accompanies by ooh's and aah's from the onlookers in the football stadium.

At midnight, the ships in the harbour hooted their horns, the deep voice of the sirens on the cruise ships sonorously gave out their deep hello to 2003, a goodbye to Funchal and that floating garden in the Atlantic Ocean that is Madeira.

The Islas Canarias

(Canary Islands)

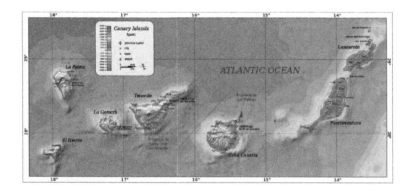

Lanzarote

Brr! It's cold outside as I write this. It has been sleeting and hail stoning and it is freezing. My thoughts turn to warm (very) lazy days in the sun, blue skies, and a sparkling turquoise sea.

There is a lot to choose from but not too far away are the Canary Islands. Some years previously, the Canary Islands started to experience a winter period where it was not as hot as hitherto. This forced us to delay our normal February birthday trip to later in the month and even into March. Thankfully, after this 'blip' normal sunshine has been restored.

There is much to choose from among the Canary Islands but Lanzarote, lying just off the west coast of Africa, has a certain appeal. It is north of Fuerteventura and the closest to Africa, being east of Tenerife and Gran Canaria. The islands also lie south of Madeira which we have visited in the last chapter. Although Fuerteventura is known for being windy we had not expected there to be so much wind in Lanzarote.

The weather on this visit was better than it had been the previous year in Tenerife but there was still a nip in the wind; that light jacket you packed may come in handy. On the other hand, it was hot, hot, hot.

An island of contrasts, with the terrain completely different to Tenerife, Lanzarote is dominated by the Timanfaya National Park and the 'Fire Mountain' – where the temperature in the ground reaches three hundred and eighty-eight degrees Celsius. It was such fun to see the experiments and cooking. I was also fascinated to see how camels got down onto the ground as they rested lazily after shedding their load of tourists.

Costa Teguise, Lanzarote. February - March 2006

The morning after our arrival I, as usual, went out to watch the sun come up. The hotel was set in gardens full of lush vegetation, palm trees and fountains rising high into the sky from cool pools of water. There was very little cloud which was such a relief after the grey skies of the UK. The air was so still at this early hour with the silence only broken by a little bird who was singing its heart out around the pool area.

Our room was a ground floor one with a terrace and a path through its own garden to the sun-lounge and pool area. The seclusion and privacy was lovely. The hotel was light and airy; in one corner was one of those huge bamboo chairs with a high curved back which of course my husband couldn't resist resting in as he recovered from the recent exertions. Although near the sea there was however, a very steep walk from the entrance down the side street to the shore. Too steep for us we found out as we contented ourselves with exploring around the area around the hotel.

Island tour.

The usual included trip took us on a day-long tour of the island which included the **Timanfaya National Park** and **Fire Mountain.** My initial impression on our first visit, was that the countryside uninspiring, flat and the land scrubby. The villages consisted mainly of non-descript low buildings.

Climbing higher, the landscape became more lunar; it felt quite eerie. There was much of evidence of lava rock as it had flowed down in the volcanic eruptions and solidified as it settled. Reaching the viewing point on the mountain the rangers treated us all to various experiments and demonstrations. They dug a hole and allowed us to hold some earth in our hands. It was so hot and as they had warned us it would do, it **burnt** the palms of our hands.

The next trick was to push a large twig into the hole and grind it into the rock. We waited for a while as it smoked and then – all at once - there was a burst of flames as it set the twigs alight as the rock was so hot. It was incredible.

The ranger then informed us that the temperature in the ground was three hundred and eighty-eight degrees Celsius. There were pipes set into the ground into which they poured water. After a short wait, the steam shot up with a **whoosh** and a **bang.** Startled, I jumped back while my husband laughed at me. He had known what was going to happen – well he would wouldn't he? The camcorder shoot went a bit haywire at that point.

Another sight was the oven set into the ground with a heat of two hundred to two hundred and eighty degrees Celsius. There was a rack on top for cooking. The guide explained that all the pipes go into the hole and hot air comes out of the pipes and up the well. Pressure builds up and hot air comes up. Each pipe is eighty degrees Celsius but as each row comes out in height the temperature increases and at the top it is two hundred and fifty degrees Celsius. A steak can be cooked in thirty-five minutes. If you want a cooler temperature for cooking it is simple – just put the food in a basket and hang it over the hole.

Our journey took us further into the mountains where we saw incredible rock and lava formations. I captured the following narrative from the guide on film,

"In some cases, the lava flowed twenty kilometres in length down to the sea. In 1730, half the population was evacuated in five months. Lanzarote suffered great devastation. There are many species of lichens and many insects of one millimetre in length. They are cave dwelling insects."

We were now in the **Valley of Tranquillity**; the lava is red and black and we saw the stalactites and stalagmites hanging from the rocks at the side of the road. As our journey took us higher into the National Park everywhere became so barren and still. At one point on the tour we were on the floor of the crater which was one hundred metres deeper than the external base.

We came down from the mountains and out of the National Park to see a line of camels lying lazily by the side of the road in the sun, resting between trips of carrying tourists. I watched carefully as another trip returned and disgorged their load. I had never known how they got down onto the ground and was fascinated to see how their back legs folded under as if jointed backwards. What an education in this unlikely place. There they lay sleepily in the sunshine blinking their eyes while chewing I know not what as they waited for their next load.

CAMELS IN TIMANFAYA NATIONAL PARK, LANZAROTE

We had earlier made a stop at a gift shop – right in the middle of nowhere- and this is where we made our usual purchase for my birthday that month. I eschewed the lovely jewellery in favour of a small tree set in black lava. The 'tree' was made up with stones of purple Amethyst (my birth stone), green Peridot (which is found in the lava rock) and orange Coral for the branches and flowers. It is a lovely reminder of our stay in Lanzarote.

César Manrique.

No writing about Lanzarote would be complete without a mention of César Manrique, a native of Lanzarote and a famous artist and architect, who had a huge influence of the development and design of the island for the tourist industry into what we see today. He had was instrumental in stopping the development of hi-rise buildings which is why the tall hotel in Arrecife is the only one on the island. It can be seen for miles around. All other buildings are low rise.

My husband took advantage of the excursion to the late artist's unique studio home in **Taro de Tahiche** where the **Fundación César Manrique** is based. He [my husband] was full of the design.

'He built his home using the bubbles that had formed in the lava flow by joining several these bubbles together using excavation tunnelling to form rooms for various uses. Basically,' he recounted, 'it is all underground.'

My husband has recalled this after ten years, so deep are his impressions.

(http://cesarmanrique.com/fundacion_i.htm 19.07.2016)

Following this visit, the tour headed towards the village of **Guatiza**, and the **Jardín de Cactus** or Cactus Garden, which again was designed by César Manrique. When he came back to the hotel, my husband was full of the amazing sights of the many cacti which are grown there but not being a botanist didn't memorize details. Therefore, he has little recall of that visit, unlike the former visit which is imprinted on his mind feeding as it did his deep interest in his engineering and discovery side.

******

Playa de los Pocillos.

Our return visit five years later took us to a lovely, flat bay just outside and to the eastern outskirts of Puerto del Carmen. Although quieter, this is how we like it. The hotel complex was two hotels joined together to form a beach club hotel. We were so thankful that we had requested a room near reception and on the ground floor as all meals, both for guests in this building and the adjoining one, were taken in this main building. One lady wore a pedometer to gauge how far she had to walk from one side to the other. We were shocked, as she was, when she told us how far it was.

The hotel gardens with their beautiful plants and secluded seating areas were beautiful and cool; tall palm trees rose into the clear blue skies. Initially, we spent some time around the pool area where the breeze caressed and played on our skin. It was a warm breeze but with a tinge of coolness at the edge.

The hotel was perfect with something for everyone including children's entertainment and activities. The extensive gardens were a pleasure to walk around to sample the refreshments and snacks from the outdoor eating area. The gardens eventually led us down a path to a secure gate from which we stepped onto the main road with the sea in front of us. Crossing the road, we entered an oasis of calm; the wide promenade and strategically placed seats offered a welcome pause and a time for quiet reflection, inviting you to gaze out the sea and the soft waves gently lapping at the shore where they met the golden sand.

The bay here curves in a wide arc around Playa de los Pocillos. It is perfect for a dip in the sea when the green flag (for safety) is flying. A quiet stroll along the promenade will lead you, if you want to venture further, to the headland around which you can see the planes coming in to land at Arrecife airport. Crossing back onto the main road, there is a small choice of hotels, bars, and cafes.

Using our special pass key gave us a secure entry back into the hotel grounds. Only for guests, mind. Back in the hotel, it was lovely to lie by the pool, or under a shady palm tree swaying in the breeze, simply chilling out only moving to have lunch or a dip in the inviting pool.

To Teguise and the Blanket Trip.

One trip on offer by the holiday company was the inevitable 'Blanket Trip'. Now you may ask yourself,

'Why do we want blankets in such a hot country?'

Good question. The answer lies in the short tour of the island on the way to the ancient capital of Teguise. The excursion was a free opportunity to see a little more of the island. Approaching Teguise, the church tower was plain to see in the distance as it rose high above the village.

Eventually we reached the sales outlet where you are introduced to the ergonomics of sleeping and what it takes to get a good night's sleep. It was an opportunity to buy a new mattress or other items which may or may not relieve discomfort. After this, we waited in the stiff breeze for our coach which would to take us to the coast and the city of Arrecife.

<u>Arrecife.</u>

As our guide explained, the only tall hotel on the island, at seventeen floors, can be seen for miles around. She explained that the famous artist and architect César Manrique, who was born in Arrecife, successfully lobbied to have planning on the island in keeping with its surroundings. The high-rise hotel does, however, give an opportunity to have a 'bird's-eye' view of the island from the seventeenth floor.

Driving down from the interior of the island we came to the city of Arrecife on the coast whereupon our driver took us past the docks and the part where the large cruise ships berth on their tour of the Canary Islands. Reaching the city centre the coach driver dropped us off at a convenient point. With a brief explanation of where we could wander at will or go into the hotel for afternoon tea on the seventeenth floor we were left to our own devices with instructions for a meet-up point later.

Heading across the plaza with its huge monuments we, along with many others, took the glass lift to the seventeenth floor. Rising steadily, we were afforded a panoramic view of all aspects of the city and the island beyond. Afternoon tea was a typical English one with cakes and a pot of tea etc. From the huge glass windows, we could see in the distance a shining white cruise ship in the harbour.

Circling around the room, we had a good view of the brilliant white modern buildings which lined the palm tree lined promenade. Although high, nothing matched the height from which we were enjoying the views.

Beyond the huddle of modern buildings of this crowded city, the mountains rose in the background. From another angle, the cruise ship lying quietly in the harbour, dwarfed the smaller boats and yachts with their masts and sails barely managing to reach the height of the first row of decks of the cruise ships with portholes above the water line.

From another angle, a sandy bay came into view, with rocky outcrops reaching out into the clear blue water where the late afternoon sunshine cast dappled shadows. Reaching the ground floor again, we could appreciate from the outside just how high was this hotel and how, if the planning regulations had not been put in place, the whole island could easily have been dominated by many others of similar height in a quest to fulfil accommodation for an emerging tourist industry. As it was, César Manrique later planned and developed much of the island sympathetically into what you and I enjoy today.

On the plaza in front of the hotel, is a sculpture consisting of a huge piece of mangled, rusty, metal on a pole. I am sure that my husband – the metal man – has an explanation so I will ask him. Hmm. No joy there, so when you visit do be sure to take note when the guide on the Blanket Trip explains it to you and do let me know.

******

Our plans to spend some quiet reading time around the pool were scuppered somewhat by a change in the weather to chilly winds and lower temperatures; unusual for February/early March. In addition, the hotel was designed around the expectation of sun, sun, sun, every day and apart from the reception area and the corridors it did not have a roof. Indeed, new arrivals were huddled in their winter jackets. Deciding to take advantage of the cooler-than-expected weather, we hired a car for two days. The hotel shop had an excellent road map with routes for tours of the north of the island and another for the south of Lanzarote. I was able therefore to capture my thoughts and impressions over the next few days on my small computer, sheltering in the covered terrace from the stiff breeze.

******

South Island tour.
To the very south of the island lies the large tourist resort of **Playa Blanca** (a short boat ride away from the neighbouring island of Fuerteventura). Although a main road leads into Playa Blanca with smaller roads to some parts nearby, on consulting our map that had the main places of interest marked, we decided to go straight across on the more minor roads to the **salt flats** and the

lagoon of **Janubio** which is a natural lake on the south-west coast. After the sea water is extracted and processed, the salt from it is eventually passed to the salt pans in the marshes. The salt flats are separated into large squares and stretch a long way into this deserted and bleak part of the island. The fishing industry requires much salt. The coast around this part of the island is very rocky with some of it needing much agility to clamber over the rocks with the most vibrant colours marking them.

Los Hervideros.

Moving on along the narrow, rocky, coast road we came to **Los Hervideros.** The day was somewhat chilly, the breeze stiff, and the coastline dramatic. Made more dramatic and deserted by its seemingly inaccessibility. Even so, it was well worth the visit to see the sea come crashing through the holes in the large rock formations that rise from the sea.

At one point, there is a natural shelf where a viewing platform appeared to have been constructed for the hardy souls who managed to scramble down to it. Not us though. We were content to look down the sheer drop into the sea and take photographs as the sea crashed and banged against the rock throwing water high into the air before falling playfully in a pool of thick white foam down below. Far, far, down below onto outcrops of rock that it washed with its never-ending ebb and flow where the blue of the water contracted with the white foam and spray.

Back in the car we drove along, all the time with a backdrop of mountains ahead. Approaching a sharp bend in the road, we were faced with a huge boulder consisting of sharp needles of rock which jutted menacingly and horizontally into the road. This part of the road was cordoned off, warning you to stay clear, which was re-assuring given that we were driving on the right side of the road and very close to this magnificent if dangerous wall of ancient, volcanic rock.

LOS HERVIDEROS – NEEDLES OF ROCK

El Golfo.

Soon, we came upon El Golfo. This crater, nestling into the volcanic rock of the cliff above, holds an emerald green lake. A beach holds the sea back and allows the eye to absorb the contrast of a deep blue sea, black volcanic sand, the deep green of the water in the crater, and the glorious colours of the cliff above. A small fishing village nearby lends an air of charm with its small whitewashed houses adorned with brilliant blue doors and gardens surrounded by stone walls. Moving on, we saw plump cactus plants nestling in the shelter of the rock by roadside and a huge bird soaring in the sky as it surveyed the scene below.

Return to Timanfaya National Park.

You will remember that I related earlier how we visited the **Fire Mountain** and the **Timanfaya National Park**. We felt that we simply had to pay a return visit and see the tricks performed by the rangers of lighting dry twigs in the volcanic earth. We also needed to look for sustenance in the shape of food.

Taking the signs and leaving the road, we slowly wound our way into the National Park absorbing the contrasts of the volcanic formations from earlier eruptions. There was a queue as the rangers would only allow so many cars in at once. Everyone was counted in and at the exit, counted out. You wouldn't want to be caught stranded overnight on that silent, barren and lunar landscape. From our previous visit, we knew that there was a cafeteria where we could buy lunch and a cool drink. Not that we needed a cool drink this time as it was quite windy to say the least. I was having a hard job keeping my skirt down.

The rangers directed us where to park; heading towards the cafeteria we once again saw the trick of lighting a fire in the heat of the volcanic earth and the demonstration where food is cooked over a huge rack covering the hole in the ground with the heat of the volcanic earth being sufficient to cook a roast dinner.

Entering the cafeteria, we were startled to be confronted by a most unusual sculpture of what looked like large frying pans attached by their handles to a pole which went from floor-to-ceiling. An unusual feature and a talking point. The frying pans I hasten to add were above head height.

Outside, visitors were experiencing the usual demonstrations, which we watched for a while but we decided to head back out, marvelling at the vibrant colours of the rock; the russets, reds, golds and black. As we were not in a special party, we were not allowed to venture where we had been on our earlier trip but were instructed to follow the signs along the road that would take us out of the National Park.

If you have the opportunity to go to Lanzarote, I can only emphasise that a guided tour is well worth the money as you get to see, and hear about, so much more from an experienced guide. Not to mention the chance for a bit of shopping in the middle of a volcano.

Towards Yaiza and La Geria.

The land was flatter now but surrounded by mountains. As we drove on, we came upon rows and rows of curved rock formations. Or should I say curved walls made up of rocks. Vines were planted in the volcanic ash and grew, sheltering in these curves, where they could hide from the wind while absorbing the full warmth of the hot sun. We were now in the valley in **La Geria** which is the wine-growing area of Lanzarote. When we were there it was March, the vines were just starting to burst forth again with leaves in the spring air.

After the beauty and starkness of the volcanic landscape around Timanfaya, it was strange to see so much greenery on the slopes of the mountains in this part of the island. It was even stranger to see a lone palm tree rising high into the deep blue sky from among the houses that we came upon. Driving through the town of **Yaiza** we didn't stop to explore but admired the cluster of white houses and the palm trees which added an air of festivity to the town.

Puerto Calero.

We had originally looked at an hotel in Puerto Calero as we were attracted to the marina but when we realized that there was a very long steep hill from the hotel to the marina, we changed our minds. Hence booking with another travel company. Now, we found ourselves quite near to this lovely marina. Our guide on the Blanket Trip had told us of its origins, and how it was an upmarket development nestling on the south-east coast but no far from Puerto del Carmen.

We drove down a quiet road and turned at the hotel, at which we had wanted to stay, down to the marina. It really was a steep hill. We didn't know if we could park on the marina front so parked quite a long way down the hill. Strolling down to the waterfront, admiring the pleasant design of the whole area, abundant with greenery and flowers, we found the marina was bordered with a nice array of shops. In the water sat the yellow submarine which took visitors out on trips into the sea.

After strolling around, resting with the inevitable ice cream and admiring the boats, we headed back to the car. We thought we had parked a long way down the hill but soon found that we had a struggle on our hands. (We were almost literally on our hands and knees.) A couple who were sitting on the wall, laughed at our discomfort. Suffice to say, that it did not quite kill us but had confirmed that we had done the right thing, for us, if choosing a hotel better placed for our limitations – to say the least.

North Island tour.

The leaflets that we had read, about the small, blind, white crabs that lived in an underground cavern on the north side of the island, had fired out imagination.

Taking advantage of the island map with detailed points of interest, we set off in the returning sunshine to explore the north of Lanzarote.

Jameos del Agua.

We quickly left the residential area of Los Pocillos, heading for the main route towards Arrecife from where the road to the north of the island leads out. The sea sparkled brightly on this pleasant winter's day. With the lower than expected temperatures, the weather was ideal for sightseeing. Although tempted to turn off and visit the **Jardin de Cactus** (Cactus Garden) we kept focused on our destination to see the little crabs in the underground grotto.

"La Cueva de los Verdes, in the northern part of Lanzarote, to the south-east of the volcano Monte de la Corona, forms part of a spectacular system of underground grottoes (the Jameos). It is not only one of the most interesting volcanic formations on the island, but is also one of the longest volcanic galleries in the world (6 km long).

"The caves and galleries were created as a result of a prehistoric eruption from the volcano Monte Corona between three and five thousand years ago, when a major stream of lava was ejected toward the east coast into in the sea."

(http://www.lanzarote.com/cueva-de-los-verdes/ 16.07.2016)

This explains it all far better than I could. However, the famous artist and architect César Manrique made the caves as we see them now.

Parking up and paying our entrance fee, we were guided to the entrance from where steps led down to the underground caverns. A profusion of hanging plants lent an air of mystery as we trod our way carefully on the rough rock. It was all so beautiful, silent, and awe-inspiring to think that these caverns were formed all those thousands of years ago, in pre-historic times.

In the middle of one was a deep lagoon. Carefully negotiating the path which went around the lagoon, we peered in the water in an effort to see the crabs. A notice extolled visitors not to throw coins into the lagoon as the 'corrosion from the coins could endanger the life of the crabs in this volcanic tube'. The notice went on to say that the crabs were called munidopsis polymorpha and were one of the world's unique species. They are also known as the blind albino cave crab.

Allen of course, was busy absorbing all he surveyed, looking carefully at the rock formation and the notices around the walls while I was ready for a rest and a cool drink. As usual, we found that the needs of visitors had not been overlooked; a café-bar had been built into the rock. All very simple with the tables and seats of wood and the menu just enough for a mid-morning snack.

From our seat in the gloom, high above the lagoon, we could see a glimpse of light through the exit from the cavern. This led out into the sunshine and, surrounded by palm trees and towering walls of dark lava, a beautiful large blue lagoon (swimming pool?). Such a contrast. Across the wide, open space was the entrance to another cavern. This cavern had been transformed into the César Manrique Underground Theatre where concerts and other events are held in the auditorium. The acoustics in there must be stupendous.

To the very northern tip of Lanzarote.

Making use of our excellent island map, we could meander across to the north-west side of the island to see the **Bateria del Rio** – a former artillery base now transformed into a restaurant and viewing platform by

César Manrique – and the **Mirador del Rio**. The area here is quite barren but looks out across the waters called **El Rio** to the small volcanic island of **La Graciosa**.

We didn't linger here but decided to meander back along the twisty minor roads to the village of **Orzola** at the very top of Lanzarote. Our recollections are that the roads were very narrow and, after driving through the village and trying to find somewhere to stop for lunch, we found a car park of sorts. It was safe. As many of the shops were closing for siesta, our choice of eatery was limited.

Wandering through the village, we came upon the harbour and the ferry. Buying a snack nearby, we settled down in the sunshine to watch the comings and goings of the ferries as we munched at our meal. Eventually, everyone was on the boat and it set off for La Graciosa. Heading back to the car park, there were fun and games in the road; it was blocked by someone wanting to make a delivery but the parked cars were an obstacle. It was all sorted out amicably and calmly. It was too hot to get worked up I expect but really, that is their relaxed way.

Back to the hotel via Costa Teguise.

Now back on the eastern side of the island, we found that the road was excellent and would lead us right past Arrecife to Los Pocillos. So off we set. Looking at the map I suggested,

'Let's go through Costa Teguise. I know we weren't impressed last time but let's just drive through.'

I am *so* glad that we did. The change that met our eyes was enormous as we slowly drove down wide tree-lined boulevards. I was totally astounded and impressed. It was obvious that a huge investment had gone into the resort as last time, I was commenting on the broken paving stones in the pavement. Not so on this visit. The wide boulevards and tastefully designed walkways and gardens were inviting. It was a pleasure to drive through the area.

Final thoughts on Lanzarote.

Our experiences in exploring this beautiful and ancient island by ourselves simply prove that, although the normal tourist attractions and wide entertainment opportunities are a magnet to many, it is well worth pushing back the boundaries a little and, with map in hand, venture out into the interior to savour a taste of what the island has to offer and a glimpse into the island traditions. If you do not have the confidence to do that, the many excursions on offer are well worth the outlay as the guides are so knowledgeable about this diverse island of contrasts.

~ ~ ~ ~ ~ ~

Fuerteventura

Clearly visible, as the plane circled its descent over the sea, was the outline of the island of Fuerteventura with its long sandy beaches and low mountains, spread out below. What a perfect retreat from the hurly burly of daily life and the harshness of a British winter.

This current escape in November had been a last-minute decision. Having visited Fuerteventura before, it was one we knew we would not regret.

Caleta de Fuste.

Fuerteventura – one of the Canary Islands – lies south of Lanzarote off the west coast of Africa. Our destination was again the small resort of Caleta de Fuste on the east coast of the island. This is a modern resort built around an old fishing village that has a marvelous sandy beach in the curved bay. In recent years, development has included the Fuerteventura Golf Resort about one kilometre south of the old fishing village. This [Golf Resort] comprises a golf course with a five-star hotel on site; there are a further three hotels across the road facing the sea. We were destined on this visit for the Elba Sara situated on one side of the huge Atlántico Centro Commercial that is filled with shops, a supermarket, cinema, amusement arcade, restaurants and cafés.

The hotel, as do the other hotels in the complex, provides a secure exit through the gardens leading straight onto the promenade. It is worth noting that for anyone with prams or mobility problems, this is a long flat promenade. A pleasant stroll in the sunshine takes you past the shopping centre, hotels and the restaurant built out into the sea. At the time, the paved part of the promenade disappeared here for a few yards at the undeveloped patch before resuming by the shops (hire your cycles here), restaurants, apartments, Thalasso Spa and tennis courts.

With two lazy camels watching as they waited for passengers, we passed along the yellow sands and sun beds of the curved bay before reaching the old fort or **'Castillo de la Caleta de Fuste'** and the **Puerto Castillo Yacht Harbour** in the old centre of the village. If you want to be a little more adventurous you can have a guided session playing with sea lions in the harbour or take part in other underwater activities on offer.

CAMELS ON THE BEACH AT CALETA DE FUSTE. FUERTEVENTURA

Continuing north around the headland, the scenery changes dramatically as the sea crashes over the rocks which form this part of the coast; here, if you are very quiet and still, you might see chipmunks as they scurry over the rocks stopping only to catch the peanuts which tourists feed them.

In our hotel, we took advantage of the all-inclusive terms on offer. Waiters transferred any left-over pastries from breakfast to the Pool Bar just in case the ample and varied choice at breakfast wasn't enough to keep you going until lunch. The Pool Bar also served snacks but only outside restaurant hours for all-inclusive guests. Afternoon tea was served in the Piano Bar with its terrace overlooking the Atlantic Ocean. It is so restful to watch the sea and listen to the waves ebb and flow. Meanwhile, the animation team attempted to keep everyone fit with a programme of activities including water aerobics demonstrated by a very fit and supple young man. Yes.

With ample sun beds the only problem was whether to roast in the sun, which would have horrified the hotel's sun care advisors, or seek some shade in the garden areas. One concern with all-inclusive holidays is a possible lack of variety between lunch and dinner menus but this wasn't the case at the Elba Sara. The chefs were to be congratulated on their imagination and variety.

Fuerteventura is noted for being windy and a favourite with surfers. However, we only experienced severe winds once on this visit. For the most part, we welcomed the occasional stiff breeze as a very welcome break to the heat of the day. If all this is not enough and you want to gorge on fast food, or the children are pining for a Big Mac, then pop across the road to McDonalds. All in all, a relaxing holiday with something for everyone.

******

Changing times mean changing considerations; the Saga holiday brochure with its detailed descriptions of terrain and location had come to the fore once again on an earlier visit to Caleta de Fuste

We had opted then for the peace of the fishing village of Caleta de Fuste, a flat and easy walk along the beach from the hotel, or a short bus ride from the Atlántico Shopping Centre next door to the hotel.

Our chosen hotel on that first visit was the Elba Carlotta – one of the three in the complex fronting the sea just a short way out of the village. It was on the other side of the Commercial Centro and the Elba Sara which I have just described.

This wonderful idyllic Hotel Elba Carlotta was set in lush gardens in which to stroll or to head straight to the back door which led onto the flat promenade. Before this first visit as I have said, friends had told us that Fuerteventura was famous for being windy. Hence the attraction for surfers. But we didn't know quite what to expect on this first visit. On our arrival, the hot sun was accompanied by very strong warm winds. I can recall from our video how windy it was; the palm trees bending into the stiff breeze as it whistled through the leaves. These lasted for the first couple of days with a lot of sand blowing across the promenade and into your face. They were very bracing if dusty. The winds eventually abated to a more manageable and welcome level. Welcome, as in the heat a breeze was pleasant.

Turning left onto the promenade to walk along the beach past the Sheraton Hotel, we passed a jetty type of walkway that led to a rotund, thatch-covered restaurant. It must be wonderful to sit in there and feel that you are in the middle of the sea.

Eventually, at one point, the beach path almost disappeared where the land [at that time] was undeveloped. Sensible shoes for negotiating through the sand, tufts of grass, and the rough path were a necessity. I am not noted as a wearer of 'sensible' shoes but really, open-toed mules are not the best choice of footwear. The road soon re-appeared in front of the few shops and cafés on the sea front where the land had been developed.

The road led around the edge of the sandy bay to the harbour and the old fishing village which lay sleepily in the sunshine. My husband always likes to stroll out before it gets too hot. Consequently, many were just coming into the world when we were out and about.

Although there are many activities on offer with some fishing, diving, and boat trips, there was little activity. However, once it wakes up after a late night, it is a very lively destination.

At the entrance to the harbour, overlooking the sea, was the old castle. We strolled along the harbour wall with its lighthouse at the end, looking at the boats moored up and the petrol/diesel pump handily situated near the mooring spots.

The little train tooted its horn as it approached the turning circle where it waited for passengers to board for a return journey through the old village and the many shops and hotels on the tree-lined streets, before crossing the main road to the complexes of apartments and villas, that were built as the area was developed to cater for the increasing number of tourists.

From the other side of the sheltered harbour the road winds northwards along the wild, rocky coast where the sea pounds with an ever-increasing force as it seeks release against the cliff face. Many apartments have been developed here with their balconies facing the sea so that holiday-makers can soak up the healing warmth of the sun's rays.

Inland are modern shops and more apartments along the tree-lined streets. Here we later collected a Boom Trike for a morning's escorted tour around the island but more of that later. The old village is now a very modern tourist destination. On the way, back from Caleta de Fuste to the hotels, we first reached the Sheraton Hotel which is very luxurious and a short step from our hotel.

We had the opportunity of experiencing a taste of this luxury when Martin, our Rep./Host that first year, invited all Saga guests to a piano recital. It was the perfect accompaniment to a relaxing Sunday afternoon. The grand piano standing in the centre of the vast foyer was impressive. With sunlight flooding through the domed high glass ceiling and surrounded by varied green plants it was so pleasant to sit with a Gin and Tonic (G&T) and listen to this talented young man treat us to a medley of classical music.

On our next, second, visit, this wasn't repeated as there was a different Rep. We did however, have free tickets for a Spa experience in the hotel where we were able to sample the different inviting pools and sauna before relaxing on the comfortable loungers. Saga had arranged this and I had the bonus of a second visit as my husband did not partake.

Turning right on the level promenade out of the hotel, we came to the well-designed entrance and seating areas on the lower floor of the Atlántico Centro Commercial (Shopping Centre) with its supermarket, café's, bowling alley, cinema and shops spread over two floors. An escalator takes you to the upper floor that in turn leads out onto the main road at the front of the three hotels. The shops have a lovely variety of goods. As usual I was drawn like a magnet to the shoe shop. You can guess the result. Carrying on past the shopping centre, you come to the third hotel in the complex – the Elba Sara [described above when a last-minute 'escape booking' wasn't possible at the Elba Carlotta].

The views from our balcony over the pool area and sea were perfect. On our arrival, it was cloudy but I recorded that,

'On returning from a walk the clouds had blown away and it was blue skies after that.' All the while as I was filming this idyllic scene, 'the surf pounded the sea shore'.

Re-playing our video as I jog my long memory makes me want to re-visit. Especially as I have the backing music of Demi Roussos singing *Island in the Sun*.

The **Jandia** peninsula in the south is famous for its long beaches. Here you will also find the **Adventure Oasis Park** with something for everyone. Suffice to say that we didn't venture out to this, preferring the peace and relaxation in our idyllic corner of the island.

Island tour.

Taking advantage of the Saga included Island Tour we looked forward to an interesting and informative day with an opportunity to learn more about the island.

Caleta Fuste lies south of the capital, Puerto del Rosario, on the east coast. Travelling on a well-maintained road we headed to the sand dunes in the north-east of the island. The coach disgorged its passengers so that they could wander over the dunes and take photos. In the distance was a large hotel on the sea shore. The coach was on a section of hard standing [tarmac]at the side of the road. The guide explained that many people came here to park up and sunbathe. The hard standing had been provided at the side of the road as many park their cars on the sand; the car wheels would then gradually sink into the soft, fine sand as the wind blows the sand against the wheels and the cars become stuck. There were two men who permanently patrolled the area to rescue stranded motorists.

Travelling northwards we could see the many clumps of vegetation in the sand. The flat sea shore was clearly visible as was the small **Isla de Lobos** which has a National Park. Eventually, as we neared **Corralejo** the island of **Lanzarote** came into view. Corralejo is very built up and the main tourist destination. Fuerteventura lies to the south of Lanzarote [they are both the closest to Africa of all the Canary Islands] and it is from Corralejo that the ferries ply back and forth the short distance between Fuerteventura and Playa Blanca on the southern shores of Lanzarote.

Turning away from the north coast, the terrain became more undulating. It appeared in stark contrast to the interior of the island of Lanzarote which we visited in the previous chapter. The earth was a glorious mix of colours from red through to green and brown as vegetation covered the sweeping fields on the mountainsides with palm trees lining the road. We were now heading down the western side of the island towards **Betancuria** which is almost on a parallel with Caleta de Fuste. On the way, we had a glimpse of **Tindaya Mountain** which was considered by the original inhabitants to be a sacred mountain.

Goat Farm and Museum near Betancuria.

Never having been to a goat farm before we had no idea what to expect. It was certainly not something we would have known about if we had been on our own. Entering the buildings, we found that we were in the museum where farm implements and all kinds of artefacts were on display. The windows of this old building were simply openings in the wall or openings covered by open slats of wood. All manner of things was on display; old clothes, a figure dressed as a farm worker would have done, an ancient battered suitcase on a bench. There were pictures of people on the rough, white walls. Who were these people? Were they of family in times gone by. It is all of interest to the visitor. Among another mix of items was a pair of old weighing scales.

Outside, Allen went to talk to the camel. Did he 'get the hump'? [Bad joke – groan.] The camel was penned in behind a low white wall in front of the covered shelter.

Inside again – I am following the sequence of the film as I wandered around – we could see many old ploughing implements. A wooden framework had material inside it of drawn thread work where sections of fabric are taken out thread by thread before being stitched together to form a pattern.

Coming to the sheds where the goats were, our guide informed us that some baby goats either had just been born or were due to be born. We were lucky enough to see a 'just born' baby goat taking its first tentative steps while its mother watched over it all the while. It always amazes me how quickly farm animals get up and go almost straight away while more domesticated animals such as cats and dogs take some time to get going. The mother goat was up and about straight away as well. No slacking there.

In another pen, other goats were waiting quietly to give birth. All the time, the air was rent with their raucous cries. The baby goats in the nursery pen had long, floppy ears. They came to the wall to be stroked by some of the visitors.

Returning to the museum part we could see a two-sided basket arrangement which would go over a camel for it to carry two people – one at each side. A framed picture on a wall titled **'Cabra Majorera. Denominacion de las Capas'** illustrated many different types of goat. The Majorera is one of the three indigenous breeds of goats.

Outside again, young goats put their front legs through the bars of the pen. Allen stroked their silky soft coats while the camel in the next pen looked on haughtily with its hooded eyes at all he/she surveyed with only its head and humps visible over the wall. All the while, the wind whistled across the open land as it came down from the mountains.

Older goats were penned nearby, their curved horns denoting their different types as they sat on the ground chewing lazily.

Down the switchback road to Betancuria and lunch.

After a hair-raising drive, down to the ancient and delightful village of **Betancuria**, we were greeted with a pictorial town sign informing us that it was 'Patrimonio Historico' which loosely translated means Historical Heritage. Betancuria, lying in the heart of Fuerteventura, was founded in the year 1404. It is the former capital of the island and now a historic monument.

We were taken to the **Craft Centre** where our guide had obtained permission for us to eat our hotel-provided picnic. Entering the Craft Centre, we came upon white-washed buildings around beautiful gardens. The tiled roofs, colourful flowering shrubs, and greenery provided a wonderful contrast.

Our first call was to a room where we were treated to a slide show about Fuerteventura, its habitats and how the land changes with the changing seasons. We saw how, after rain, a wonderful array of colourful plants pushed their way through the seemingly barren soil to greet the sunshine.

Outside again, a medley of buildings housed different crafts. At one, an old man sat between two huge lidded wicker baskets as he concentrated with knotting or plaiting long strips of fabric while inside an array of crafts vied for space. Numbers and letters on tiles were displayed on the rough-hewn door. A frame of wood nearby gave a hint of what the man was up to was up to.

A bar area served coffees that you could enjoy at one of the many shaded tables or on one of the seats set among the plants and flowers while you consumed your packed lunch. This usually consisted of a bread roll, cheese, ham, pot of dessert and/or fruit. Allen delved into our bag of goodies to choose a big juicy orange.

Colourful geraniums of red and mauve flowered profusely. One part of the garden was given over to a display of cactus plants. Everywhere was coolness, quiet and beauty as the glorious profusion set off the red-tiled walkways and terracotta pots. The gardens of the Craft Centre looked out to the mountains and rolling countryside. One craft stall had great 'wheels' of goat's cheese. These large circular slabs of cheese were covered in some kind of white stuff. Pictures behind showed the timeless scene of a man sitting on a stool as he milked a goat. Farm implements decorated a white-washed wall of one of the buildings.

Coming out of the Craft Centre we came to the town square. The long low walls of the pretty white-walled church bordered one side while on another, a building had typical Canarian balconies. Huge lettering reading BAR sat high on the wall near the roof. A tourist sat on a stone bench in quiet contemplation. It was a timeless scene set off by the fat palm tree dominating the centre of the square. Palm trees dotted around swayed in the breeze as birds chirruped among their leaves. A wonderful, traditional old town nestling in the lava rock of the surrounding mountains.

High above the church roof a bell tower housed two very old bells. The corner walls were faced with red bricks (lava bricks?). These contrasted with the brilliant white of the walls. Inside, the simplicity of the architecture was offset by the rich intricacy of the altar screen and the Bishop's seat behind the cloth-covered altar.

The journey across the island back to Caleta de Fuste took us through land that is so different to other Canarian islands. It is as if the lava has flowed down from different directions to meet in the middle and form folds in the hills. The land appeared more barren but with farms and villages dotted about. A most wonderful day, part of which we had the opportunity to repeat on our next Saga visit when beautiful Betancuria was again on the itinerary. What a treat.

******

I said earlier that we visited a third time but stayed at the Elba Sara on the other side of the Centro Commercial. At the airport, we espied David, who had been our Saga Rep. in Nerja a few years earlier. We went to visit him at the Elba Carlotta whereupon we took advantage of an early booking discount and booked a long-awaited tour to the south of Italy.[ii]

******

Aloe Vera Factory.

A visit to the Aloe Vera Factory on Fuerteventura is a must. Situated in the south of the island, the factory is simply a long building among the surrounding desert-like land. Surprisingly, we learned that the Aloe Vera plant is not from the cactus family as we thought due to its fleshy leaves, but from the lily family. The subsequent demonstration took us through the preparation and processing of the plant. The demonstrator showed us how the leaves of the plant are opened and the juicy flesh scraped off in a carefully skilful way.

We also learned that only *fresh* aloe vera added to other products as a beneficial ingredient, is beneficial. Once it is dried, it loses its active properties. There was a demonstration on willing visitors to have some of the gel massaged into their necks and experience the benefits of high quality aloe vera.

Naturally, products are on sale – what would be the point of the visit if not? We did buy a small amount but on arrival home we purchased more by fax once we needed new supplies. A pleasant afternoon.

The Boom Trike Adventure.

We spurned the usual cycle, motorcycle, scooter, and car rental options. Allen wanted to hire a Boom Trike as, not only had he seen a programme on television about them, he was having withdrawal symptoms at leaving his beloved Gold Wing motorcycle at home. The television programme had given details of where you could hire one of these. Naturally, we carefully noted details for future reference. In our hotel reception area, the information book included a **Cool Runnings** leaflet about the Boom Trike experience and how we could book. Taking the plunge, one very sunny morning off we went into Caleta de Fuste, donned our little steel hats and climbed aboard for a guided tour into the mountains.

Being up early, I did my usual thing and stood on the balcony to catch the atmosphere of the early morning on film.

'It is Saturday morning and we have got up very early to have breakfast and then we will go to Caleta de Fuste to collect the trike that we have hired for the day. I think it will be a guided tour of the island but in any case, Allen is going to be at the helm as usual. It looks set to be another glorious day. Just a little wind but it is coming from the south anyway which means it is very, very, warm.'

As I panned the camcorder over the pool area from my vantage point on our balcony, I continued,

'It is about twenty past eight and there is very little sign of life.'

Now, after walking into the village, we found ourselves outside the **Cool Runnings Trike Tours** office and showroom. The Cool Runnings experience can be either by chauffeur or self-drive, in which case you are guided from the front by another trike. John, the owner, took us around his showroom and 'talked' bikes with Allen. One trike was dressed out in stars and stripes. It transpired that this was to be ours for the day. John explained another 'which is using a smart engine and quite high tech'.

Kitted out with crash helmets, we found ourselves out in the sunshine after John had pushed the trike through the folding doors of the showroom onto the paved area outside. Allen listened carefully as John explained how the indicators, gears and brakes worked. (As I played this film through, Allen said that if I played anymore I would be wanting one. I think that he meant himself.)

Outside was another trike with double rear seats for two passengers.

'That is the one I will be using,' John explained.

As I waited patiently and with mounting excitement, I commented to the film,

'We are going up in the mountains, near where we were on the Island Tour last week. The sun is getting up really high now.'

After climbing aboard and getting comfortable, Allen negotiated the ramps in front of the showroom onto the road. He was cautious as he got the feel of the trike, carefully keeping our guide in sight. I had the opportunity to film the area as we passed the bay, rode onto the long straight road ahead and headed into the mountains. From my perch behind Allen, I had a good view of all the dials on the trike – not least keeping my eye on the speed dial.

The land at either side of the road at this point was flat; the distant mountains forming a wonderful backdrop. Passing through a village with the road bordered by palm trees we headed into the mountains where the earth changed colours and white villages dotted the area. Bowling along it was exhilarating to feel the warm breeze on our faces as, climbing higher we turned onto a road that a coach couldn't navigate. Eventually, we came to a high point with excellent views over the island and, of course, a café.

Amazingly, clumps of flowering plants, in complete contrast to the seemingly barren land surrounding them, had poked their way through the soil. We felt as if we were on top of the world. Incongruously, against this backdrop of volcanic eruptions and nature, the paved road leading to the café and viewing point sported very modern lamp-posts. Looking out over the valleys, it was clear to see the minor roads that followed the path of the mountain terrain; they were like ribbons that had been flung into the air and had come to rest in haphazard confusion.

THE BOOM TRIKE ADVENTURE

The ride downhill was even more exhilarating and exciting than the ride up as we followed the switchback road down to the coast. We hadn't had so much fun since our Gold Wing motorbike adventures in Andorra and Spain some years previously. Riding now through a town the church looked familiar. Was it Betancuria? Antigua? Possibly not Betancuria as not only was it in the opposite direction to where we needed to go but the bell tower looked different. Travelling on remote roads we saw the island from a different perspective on this exciting tour.

I got some good shots on film but am not sure how I managed to film Allen's face upside down and got a shot right up his nose. In a manner of speaking that is but also in actual fact. Work that one out for yourself. I probably forgot which way I was holding the camcorder.

Eventually, we reached Caleta de Fuste. It was the end of a wonderful adventure which also assuaged Allen's withdrawal symptoms at not having his beloved Gold Wing motorbike/trike to ride on these wonderful roads.

It was also the end of a wonderful stay in the island of Fuerteventura. *(I have been informed by my beloved, that if we ever visit Fuerteventura again, we will have another boom trike experience but that I will be at the front.)*

On later visits as we continued to escape to the sun, we were content to simply relax and wander at will allowing the sunshine to melt away the stresses and strains of life.

~ ~ ~ ~ ~ ~

Gran Canaria

Although we have visited the Canary Islands many times – most visits being to Tenerife but latterly to Lanzarote and Fuerteventura – we had never visited Gran Canaria. As with other Canary Islands, the island lies in the Gulf Stream off the west coast of Africa, but between Fuerteventura to the north-east and Tenerife to the north-west. It is rounder in shape than the others with all the valleys and rivers flowing out from the mountains high in the centre of the island. This makes for some dramatic scenery.

With a very special wedding anniversary looming, we wanted to continue family celebrations with a sunshine holiday. After looking at the description of our holiday experience and checking the terrain layout on the Internet we eagerly anticipated our two-week relaxing stay at the beach hotel Dunas Don Gregory. This proved an excellent choice as it lay at the southern end of San Agustin with direct access to the long promenade which swept around the sandy bay onwards to the more built up Playa Del Ingles – so called as a famous English pirate was buried on the beach (so we were told).

The weather was good to say the least. Strolling along to the northern end of San Agustin we came to a rocky coast where little crabs lay in the Spring sunshine. My husband, always keen to watch these, was busy snapping away.

As well as lazing in the sunshine and enjoying the all-inclusive hospitality of the hotel, we booked onto a couple of e so that we could see something of the island. Unfortunately, the excursion to the capital Las Palmas de Gran Canaria did not materialise but we did enjoy a full day tour to the interior of the island where we ventured high into the mountains.

POSTCARD ©EDICIONES A.M. ANDRES MURILLO S L.

With an easy connection from San Agustin to the motorway we were soon heading north-east towards Las Palmas. Skirting what looked to be a very busy city, we carried on along the north coast.

Arucas and Rum Distillery.

Our first stop was the Arucas Rum Distillery just outside Arucas (Arehucas). Faced with row upon row of barrels full of rum, we were amazed to see the ends of the barrels covered in signatures. Many were from many famous people and dignitaries – even the King of Spain.

After touring the various processes of bottling and packing we were led to the inevitable shop where a long counter was covered with bottles of all kinds of rum. I am not a rum drinker but did try the 12-year-old one. Mm. It was so smooth, so warming.

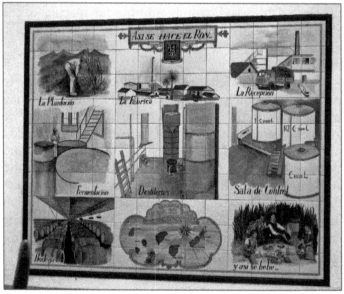

RUM DISTILLING PROCESS – ARUCAS . GRAN CANARIA.

Then we went on to sample banana rum, and chocolate rum, both of which I declined. Turning back for a sample of a normal rum, I was faced by a scrum of people with arms outstretched, reaching for the bottles which – by this time – had been left unattended for us to sample at will. The picture shows the process of rum making.

Soon we arrived in the old town of Arucas where, in a very old church silence was ruled to be golden. Afterwards, we found a coffee shop in one of the old buildings nearby.

Teror.

The mountains rose high as we traversed valleys along switchback roads. Las Palmas was visible in the distance from our viewpoints. Teror is a typical Canarian village with those fantastic ornate wooden balconies. Finding a gift shop, I browsed happily into the far reaches of the building while my husband waited outside in the fresh air and shade.

Valleseco.

Climbing ever higher towards the clouds we came to our planned lunch stop in Valleseco. Our guide had related to us on the coach the choice of meals so that we could choose and she could ring ahead with the choices. Wine or other drinks were included with the meal and soon, replete and comfortable we headed further inland to the centre of the island. There was some very good planning in our journey times as all day we found that our party was the first one at a stop therefore we were leaving as all the other coaches were arriving.

Tejeda and Ayacata.

The roads wound higher and higher providing an ever-changing scene. At some viewing points of nearly one thousand five hundred feet high you could clearly see Las Palmas. Heading south towards **Ayacata**, the **Roque Nubio** in the distance towered high into the sky. If it had been a clear day, our guide told us, we would have been able to see Mount Teide which dominates Tenerife.

<u>San Bartolome de Tirajana and the coast</u>.

It was getting cooler now in the mountains when we made our last comfort stop. Then, our route took us south to **San Bartolome** as, gradually, we made a hair-raising, stunning, and spectacular descent down the mountains to the motorway, the coast and our hotel. What a brilliant day we had had.

Puerto De Mogan.

Our half day excursion to Puerto De Mogan would follow the coast road westwards from San Agustin. This coast road ends at Puerto De Mogan from where it turns north to follow the valleys and over the mountains to the west side of the island. Until recently the motorway ended at Puerto Rico further east but the new tunnels through the mountains have made travel much easier; this was the route home.

Early one morning, we boarded our coach to head towards Maspalomas from where we could see the sand dunes and the **Faro de Maspalomas** or (Lighthouse). This coast road took us through the villages of **Arguineguín** and **Puerto Rico** with its busy harbour/port where, from our vantage point of the coach high on the road on the side of the mountain, we could see the many boats. Once in Puerto De Mogan, looking back and upwards we could see how high on the side of the mountain we had been. Almost hanging off with a sheer drop to one side. It is a fascinating way to get a good glimpse of the coastline and geography of the area.

Our guide gave us the choice of heading off ourselves or following her to the harbour. What an enchanting place. There were many boats in the harbour and the bustle of market day did not detract from the tranquil scene. We were both entranced by the streets where walls and bridges across the streets were festooned with flowering shrubs of many colours as they rambled at will.

PRETTY PUERTO DE MOGAN. GRAN CANARIA.

After enjoying a crêpe (pancake) with ice cream at one of the many cafes we strolled through the market back to our collection point for a swift journey through the long (two kilometre) mountain tunnels on the motorway back to San Agustin for lunch. If you think that the Canaries are all sun sea and sand – think again. I hope that I have dispelled that perception entirely.

Return to Gran Canaria. Another escape to the sunshine.

This well-timed visit to San Agustin, set on a lovely sandy bay on the south-eastern coast of Gran Canaria, was an escape from the snow and ice of the UK where everyone was slithering and sliding about. We, on the other hand, were basking in the warmth of the winter sunshine of the Canary Islands.

Staying again at the Dunas Don Gregory on the beach we truly relaxed while enjoying the facilities of this wonderful hotel. **San Agustin** was the major resort until the Maspalomas area was developed. Now, this area is quieter and utterly charming. With direct access to the promenade you can walk along to Maspalomas or, you can turn left and walk along the mix of rocky coast and sandy beaches to the town itself. It is a pleasant stroll with an option of turning inland to meander through the park.

One day – one of the rare days when I moved myself off the sun bed or sunny pool terrace – we were entranced at the antics of two green cockatoos and two doves which flitted about. I think that the cockatoos were nest-building as one was tearing away furiously at a dead twig on a bush.

I enjoyed the frequent fashion shows in the pool area of beach and casual wear. The night-time shows featured items from the Italian boutique in the hotel. I promise you that I was very strong-minded when browsing in there. I only spent a little.

On our first visit two years previously, we did take advantage of the tour of the island and the visit to the beautiful **Puerto De Mogan**. This time around we had decided that we wouldn't go on any excursions as complete relaxation was on the menu. The only downside was that we both came out in streaming colds which took some time to get over. Quite a few people were also suffering, so it must have been something in the air. Fortunately, there was a good Farmacia in the Centro Commercial near the hotel – as well as good red wine in the hotel bars and the restaurant which overlooked the sea.

I thought that it would either kill the germs or drown them.

C'est la vie!

La Gomera

The small and mysterious island of La Gomera – the second smallest of the Canary Islands at about fifteen and a half miles (twenty-five kilometres) in diameter east to west – lies to the west of Tenerife. No visit to Tenerife would be complete without at least one journey by ferry to this beautiful island.

Out to sea by ferry.

With the ferries sailing from the harbour at Los Cristianos on the west coast of Tenerife, it was impossible to turn down the opportunity on one of our early visits to Los Cristianos, to explore. Despite Allen's reservation about a boat crossing, he was anxious to see the island and agreed to the trip.

As usual, I loved to film the early morning rising sun and the sky as it turned red over the horizon.

'It is now a quarter to eight o'clock and the sky is quite light. At a quarter past seven this morning it was pitch black. We got up quite early this morning as we are going to the island of La Gomera. You can just see it in the distance over there about twenty-four miles away (thirty-eight kilometres) and we believe that it is completely unspoilt. There isn't an airport there yet [1996] but I believe that one is under construction.'

'It is going to be a full day today and we are quite looking forward to it. There is the moon just going to bed.' (I was filming a white spot in the sky.) 'Across the harbour, boats at anchor are dotted here and there and by the harbour wall. The large white shape is of the ferry waiting for us.'

Arriving at the harbour after a short stroll from the hotel and with boats still lying at anchor in the water, our ferry was getting ready for sailing time with its radar swinging around at the top of a structure. Allen settled himself outside while I scurried along the boat to explore.

The island of Tenerife receded as the boat ploughed through the water with white foam left in the wake of the ship. The rising sun shone down onto the water, a portent of a good day ahead. The peak of Mount Teide on Tenerife dominated the skyline. It was very windy at sea but as La Gomera came into view, the green hills rising above the coast came clear, as did the cluster of houses around the harbour below a sheer rock face.

Leaving the ferry at San Sebastian on La Gomera, we boarded the coach which would take us to see parts of the island. Mount Teide on Tenerife is the highest point in Spain at twelve thousand feet (over three thousand metres). At every twist and turn on the mountain roads, snow-capped Mount Teide was in our sight. Down below we could see the settlements in the valleys.

The south of the island is very green. The winding mountain road took us through this lush and fertile land. Higher, we saw barren rock from lava flow, cacti, and ferns. We were now in the **Parque National de Garajonay** where, at one point, we stopped at a viewing platform. From here the fertile fields spread themselves out before us. **La Laguna Grande** in the centre of the island was misty.

After an early start that morning we were ready for lunch. Everything was ready for us at the Las Rosas restaurant that served typical food from La Gomera. The restaurant was in a huge modern building. Red checked tablecloths covered the tables while carved wooden chairs lent a traditional air as did the low beamed ceilings. The openings in the walls were simply large windows to provide a frame for the marvellous views outside, while the rough walls were simply white-washed.

After lunch, we were treated to a demonstration of the old method of communication on La Gomera. This was a special kind of whistling called *el silbo* by which the natives sent their message across the valleys. They talked by whistling through their fingers. One waiter stood at one side of the room and whistled to another at the other side who answered with a tuneful whistle. They announced:

'White Wine. Vino Blanco.' Followed by,

'Rose Wine. Vino Rosado.' Then,

'Red Wine. Vino Tinto.'

After each announcement, the other waiter would say it in whistles.

Afterwards we went out onto the mountainside terraces of Las Rosas from where we had fantastic views; Mount Teide in the distance was still clearly to be seen. After looking at the old weaving sheds and looms we boarded the coach for the journey back to the bustling harbour in San Sebastian. Here, we had some time to wander around and gather together as we waited for the ship.

Speeding away from the island, La Gomera and the green clad mountains which swept down to the sea receded into the distance as Tenerife appeared. Allen stood quietly by the rail of the ship in the sea breeze. A wonderful day.

Another visit, another experience.

In 2017, we returned to Tenerife after a gap of ten years. Our holiday company this time was Saga Holidays who offered an excursion to La Gomera as an optional extra. My research on the Internet gave details of the fast ferry service, which in the event our Saga Rep. booked for us through another company. The Saga excursion was by the normal ferry.

The pick-up time was at seven-fifteen in the morning. Yes, so early. The hotel allowed us to pre-book an early continental breakfast. Eventually a coach arrived to collect us and another couple from outside the hotel. The guide explained that we would go to Las Americas and transfer to another coach. This would then take us on a short journey to Los Cristianos.

Our guide for the day was a Belgian man called Bernard. The coach was full of people of mixed nationalities. Undaunted, Bernard amazingly went on to explain everything three times in three different languages.

The fast ferry sat huge and imposing in the waters of Los Cristianos harbour.

'The ferry Benchijigua Express is according to Lineas Fred Olsen is the largest fast ferry in the world. It goes from Los Cristianos on Tenerife to San Sebastian de la Gomera.

The comfortable trimaran ferry Benchijigua Express was built in 2005. It is a about 125 meters long and can carry 1291 passengers as well as 341 cars.'
(Source http://www.gomeralive.com/ferry-fred-olsen/ 24.03.2017)

With a ferry the size of three football fields it certainly was large; so large that with all the cars and coaches you wonder how it can simply sit on the water as it churns its way across to its destination.

Leaving the coach at the ferry terminal, we gathered as instructed ready to pass through Passport Control. This was uneventful and we soon mounted the gangplank whereupon we then found that we had to climb two steep flights of steps. Agility is the operative word to say the least.

The crossing was very smooth on the huge, high-speed trimaran. With ample, comfortable, seating inside there was also room at the rear for people to be buffeted by the breeze as the ferry ploughed through the smooth Atlantic waters. I tried to get some film of the approach to the island but it was very windy. Slowly, we watched land come into view. Firstly, the humps of the mountains before slowly, a splash of white denoting habitation became apparent, and then the buildings climbing up the mountain above the capital – San Sebastián de la Gomera.

I had wondered how, if the ferry sailed straight into the harbour, we could disembark from the rear. We would get wet surely? My husband explained that the ferry could turn around in the water and then back-up to the harbour wall. Basically, it could spin around slowly on its own axis. This it did and came to a stop right beside the colourful array of boats moored in the marina of the Punta de San Cristobal. The port is one of the places that Christopher Columbus stopped off at on his way to his discoveries of the New World many years ago.

Arriving in the harbour on the south of the island we followed Bernard's instructions to disembark on the correct side – otherwise we would get wet as we fell into the water – and make our way to the meeting point by the ferry terminal building. From there we would be able to board the coach which had also crossed on the ferry.

The plan was to drive through the tortuous mountain roads to the north of the island, stop for lunch at Las Rosas, then make our way south through the National Park of Garajonay before arriving back at the harbour. Here we would have some free time to explore before the meeting time for the journey back.

You will remember that I described earlier how, at every twist and turn, you could see Mount Teide on Tenerife as it dominated the skyline. In the intervening years, many of the bends in the mountain roads had been improved. However, as it was impossible to straighten out the bends on these narrow roads, many long tunnels had been bored through the mountain. At one point, during an open side of one tunnel, you could see the now disused old road and the grass growing through the tarmac.

Although it was a shame that we did not see much of El Teide, the journey certainly through the Valle de Hermigua was smoother and safer.

Nearing the north of the island, Bernard pointed out the mountain village of **Hermigua** down below in the valley. We now had an unexpected stop as the coach turned off the main road to descend steeply into the village. The coach disgorged its load on the narrow street as the side of the convent and the steep cobbled road which led down to the church and beyond. A plaque on a wall by the church celebrated four hundred years of the convent.

A PLAQUE CELEBRATING FOUR HUNDRED YEARS

The small church was cool and dim inside. There was much carved wood and steps up to a balcony at the back. Such a lot of steps. After a look around, and a short explanation for those interested, we made our way out to the blistering sunshine and slowly, very slowly, hauled ourselves up the steep narrow road using the pipe which was nailed to the side wall of the convent as a handrail. Bernard had jokes that they don't have fitness classes here. They don't need them. It certainly was a workout.

Driving on, our journey through the village took us past palm trees and many small banana plantations. At one point, we could see crates of green bananas being loaded from the small warehouse onto a lorry ready for despatch.

Once again, we came to the restaurant of Las Rosas. This restaurant had many tables laid out for the expected guests from coach parties. Plates containing – you guessed it – bananas, were ready for the addition of a tub of creamy dessert at the end of the second course. Squashing into our chair, we found ourselves opposite a charming Belgian couple. They spoke good English, as they all do, and we had some stilted communication. Later, we would have a longer conversation at the ferry port as we waited for passport control.

Our meal consisted of a delicious vegetable soup served from a large tureen. The second course was chicken or fish. Choosing chicken, I found that it was so well cooked that I could not break the hard surface. Apart from which, it was a leg and I am not keen on that preferring the whiter meat of the chicken breast. Wine and water accompanied this simple meal.

Once again, we were treated to a 'whistling' demonstration. Bernard had explained that it is now compulsory on La Gomera for children to learn the language in school so that it does not die out. Bernard gave the instructions to the whistler who answered with the unique responsive way. He also asked one of the party to ask an unscripted question so that we could see how genuine it all was.

There was time after this to go onto the terraces and soak up the sunshine and the timeless views of the fertile valley and the surrounding mountains.

The following drive south took us into the **Parque Nacional de Garajonay**. Entering the park to where we could admire the flora and fauna on the way to a cool clearing, Bernard explained that the plants were protected and that it was forbidden to take anything away. He explained this sternly as one of the group tried to take off a few leaves.

At various points along the pathway, there were descriptive plaques of the flower we were looking at. This was a lovely botanical surprise; both to see this developed visitor centre and to have the plants explained. After ice cream from the café (me) we continued our way descending the mountains to San Sebastian once more. This time we were approaching from the west, giving us a different aspect and views as we twisted and turned around the bends.

There was, as promised, time to explore and Bernard pointed out the main shopping streets. We, as is our want these days, settled for a cool drink and headed to the excellent café in the ferry terminal building.

As we queued up for the ferry, we once again started chatting to the Belgian couple. We had been advised to have our passport or ID card ready for inspection and swiping into the handheld terminal that the officer used. They noticed that we did not have an ID card and were intrigued, whereupon we showed them the front of our unique red passport. As we had visited Belgium, and more importantly Bruges, we had something in common to discuss which was good.

Arriving back at Los Cristianos harbour we found that there was not a change of coach on the way back but that we would be dropped off at our hotel along with the others. As our hotel was the furthest out we found ourselves at number eleven in the queue, after Las Galletas, as those in the main resorts were dropped off first.

After an early start, it certainly was a long if satisfying day. One not to be forgotten.

Tenerife

The beautiful and diverse island of Tenerife is the last of the islands that we are visiting in *Island Interludes*. The only two that we have not visited are the smaller islands of La Palma and El Hierro which both lie to the west of the archipelago. Tenerife, the largest of the Canary Islands, is an isosceles triangular-shaped island with lush, green mountainous terrain in the north that gives way to the more barren coast and hot temperatures in the south.

Tenerife lies to the east of the islands of La Palma and El Hierro and north-east of the island of La Gomera a short ferry ride away which we explored in the last chapter.

Our first visit to Tenerife was with our close friends Joan and Rob; it was a journey into the unknown. Hiring a car, we explored the island to the full and what a wonderful introduction to this stunningly, beautiful island.

Being quite new to this travel game and having just taken ownership of the camcorder which I had won for my husband in a product knowledge competition, who in the event was happier with a still camera, I spent a lot of time filming all manner of things going on in the airport. After all, that is where our holiday began.

On looking back on the film, now transferred to DVD, I was astonished at the changes that we have witnessed in the intervening years. Then, it looked empty compared to the crowded hustle and bustle of today. All these inconsequential things that I filmed at the time have now come into their own as I use this detail for authenticity in my writings.

Our men handled check-in at the airport while we ladies, knowing our place, stepped back as we waited with the hand luggage until all procedures were complete. Taking our seats on the aircraft, I settled beside the window. Is it my imagination or were the windows larger then? In those days, I was so excited I filmed everything including the take-off, the clouds, and even how the flaps on the wings moved. In fact, anything that moved.

The pilot relayed our flight route details telling us that,

'The flight will be three hours forty-five minutes. We will be flying at twenty-nine thousand feet.'

Surely today the flight is more like four hours and thirty-five minutes long?

Approaching Tenerife, the lie of the land spread out below us in a cloudless blue sky while the sea sparkled and lapped the shore.

'Can you see Teide on your left?' asked our friends from their seats in front of us. Teide was snow-capped even in June. As the plane circled to approach from the south the green vegetation of the north gave way to a more barren appearance. Touchdown was smooth.

This holiday had been a last-minute booking where we had been given little option of where to stay, eventually arriving in anticipation at our hotel in the new development of Playa Paraiso on the south-western side of the island. It was one of three hotels, very comfortable, with little else around amid the otherwise undeveloped volcanic land [1993] with a rough road to the main road. Hence the hire car later. The hotel faced the sea. It was a sun trap where, from our balcony which also faced the sea, I had fun and games with the camcorder as I zoomed in to all around us such as a cruise ship on the horizon.

The entertainment was excellent and nothing like we had seen before with flamenco dancing involving much stamping of feet and clicking of castanets; sipping large cocktails we watched the snakes in a basket and a slick magician. The hotel shop tempted us with a most beautiful display of embroidered linen.

Joan and Rob, our friends, had visited the island previously and were anxious to show us some of the sights. Firstly, we walked down the road to catch the bus which would take us through the mountain village of Adeje to the main resort of Playa de las Americas further south. The ride to Adeje was a trial for my husband as the twists, turns, and rocking of the bus as it ground its way upwards was not a happy time for a bad traveller. We found this area very built up.

Coming to Playa de las Americas, as warned, we found that the sand was black. It was of course volcanic sand. We ladies paddled in the sea, jumping the surf as we tried to keep our shorts dry. Wandering along the palm tree fringed promenade, we had a good view of the brave people who were either paragliding or riding the waves on a jet-ski.

The African couple trying to sell their wares were very colourful in their traditional robes. Don't forget that the Canary Islands are just off the west coast of Africa. Along the edge of the promenade we were fascinated to see palm trees growing in the sand, flowering cactus plants and the straw sunshades under which sunbathers could keep cool.

As I have said, there was very little around the new development where we were staying. In fact, there was nothing. The solution therefore, was to hire a car. My husband had not driven abroad before but fortunately, Rob drove for a living and had no qualms about driving on the 'other' side of the road. They gave us an introduction to Tenerife that we would never have had if we had been on our own. Consequently, we fell in love with its diversity, culture, sun, and history.

Day 2 tour.

On the first day of hire, we drove around the south of the island to the north. Stopping briefly at the Plaza in **Candelaria** to look at the ornate church against the sea, we headed on with a coastal drive to **Santa Cruz de Tenerife**. This is the capital of the island and the main port. We found it heavy with traffic. Along the palm tree lined main coastal road we saw, many big boats, huge cranes, and tall buildings that were enhanced by lovely flowering trees. Many years later we were to see a great contrast in the new developments around the harbour area.

Stopping to rest on the Avenida Francisco la Roche, we noticed the bust of Francisco Morazán, a famous Honduran politician 1792–1842. The huge clock nearby told us that it was twenty-five minutes to twelve o'clock whereupon the two couples went separate ways for lunch and shopping.

Later, travelling on with a backdrop of mountains we were entranced to see a lady in the University city of **La Laguna**, balancing a box of goods on her head as she crossed the busy road. She steadied it with one hand until, safely across among the traffic, she let go and simply walked with a very straight back and perfect balance as if to say, 'Look, no hands.'

The square in La Laguna is very cool with seats strategically placed under shady trees. As we sat in this cool square with fat pigeons pecking away nearby for crumbs we commented,

'Look, how green that mountain is over there.'

La Laguna is inland in the northern part of the island between the north and south coasts of that north-eastern tip which just out into the sea. This former capital of Tenerife and second most important city lies in the Aguere Valley, surrounded by the mountains of this verdant part of the island.

Driving down a busy and very long street and passing a yellow post box, a bus made up of two sections quietly and elegantly made its way through the city. We had not seen a bus like this before. Reaching the north-west coast via the motorway we could see the top of Mount Teide peeking through the clouds.

Soon, driving down narrow streets, we came to the harbour and the tree-lined square of **Puerto de la Cruz**. Enjoying a cool drink at a café in the square, Rob commented in satisfaction,

'Aren't we lucky?' We were.

Many children, splashing with shrieks and laughter in the water, cooled off in the shallow part of the harbour; the boats that were pulled out of the water did not deter the bathers. Some of the fishing boats were moored just a little further out of the harbour. It was a happy scene.

The north coast here is wild as the Atlantic breakers charge at the sea wall before retreating into the ocean. Huge squares of concrete acted as a breakwater. In the harbour, a fisherman was trying his luck.

Back on the road at almost two o'clock and travelling along the north-west coast, we were driving through a very green area with lots of trees. Seeing a sign for San Francisco we commented laughingly, 'Phew! What a trip we have had.'

I captured the commentary which ran between the four of us.

'This is where we got lost.'

'Don't be silly, we are not lost'

'Yes, we are.' (Even today we ladies say that, 'We got lost,' and the men reply, 'We weren't lost, you can't get lost.')

We were not on a motorway but were on a mountain road with the sea on our right.

'It is quite chilly. About three thousand feet up.' I was looking at my AA Guide Book on the Canary Islands.

'They've got weeds. What are they doing with those weeds?'

'Feeding the cow in the shed?' Was one suggestion.

Such relief when we came to a junction and hit the main road. We had a choice. The sign pointing to the left told us that we could go to,

'Santiago del Teide 4km. and Guia de Isora 19km.' or, to the right we could go to, 'Santa Cruz 73km.' which is where we had just come from. We had certainly come over a mountain.

Apparently, we had taken a 'diversion' from the coast road somewhere around **Icod de los Vinos** that took us high through the **Las Hiedras** mountains with the sea on our right. As we were all used to the mountain roads of North Wales [UK] these roads were not a problem. It is just that we got lost.

Yes. We did.

It was getting late in the afternoon with low cloud on the mountain. Taking the sign for **Santiago del Teide** we turned left and headed down into the sunshine and our hotel.

It was pleasant in the evening to sit with friends, listening to the keyboard player/singer, the games, and professional shows, mulling over the day as we laughed at the antics of the competitors in the party games.

Day 3 tour.

Next morning, outside the hotel again was a time-share tout offering us a car for two days if we went to a presentation. We good-naturedly joined in the banter exchanging where we all came from. With a promise that,

'If it rains in the morning we will go,' we took our leave.

'How much did you pay for the car?' The man was persistent.

'Eleven thousand pesetas.'

He assured us that he could have got us one for six thousand pesetas and let us go on our way as he waited for his next prospective client.

Today we were off to **Mount Teide or El Teide**. Leaving the bright sunshine of the south behind we headed through the southern slopes of the crater through low cloud. The journey took us up well-maintained roads and pretty, white villages. The mountain was clothed in rich vegetation and many trees. Climbing higher, the clouds looked to be on a level and then below our line of sight as we broke through to the blue sky above. The tops of trees were level with banks of fluffy cotton wool-like clouds.

The terrain changed now. It was lava.

'How can you tell?' I asked.

'There is nothing growing on it,' someone replied.

Our friends had been before so we were happy to be guided by them, plus they were happy to drive. Now, in the Teide National Park, we could see the peak and,

'Can you see where the lava has come down?'

We were told that it was to be five years before it erupted again. Tall, jagged, perpendicular rocks sat among the apparent wasteland. A cable car came into our line of sight. Reaching the cable car station at the base of Teide, we were at two thousand three hundred and seventy metres. The cable car takes you higher to three thousand five hundred and fifty-five metres (eleven thousand six hundred and sixty-three feet) at **La Rambleta** from where you can walk to the summit.

Setting off early in the morning meant that we had arrived before most of the coach parties and long queues. Buying our tickets for the cable car, the ticket man cautioned us,

'Can't stay longer than one hour afterwards.'

Taking deep breaths and with some excitement tempered by trepidation we soon boarded and found a place near the windows. Slowly we trundled up the mountainside; the parked coaches and cars were far below, looking like toys. With a shake, bump, and rattle when the car hit the cable connections higher up, laughing shrieks and calls of 'oooh!' rent the air.

The land below us was a variety of colours, some of it black and barren as the outline of the coast far below lay before us. With a last bang and rattle the cable car slid gently into the station where a group of passengers were waiting to board for the journey down.

An information board displaying a drawing of the area informed us that we were at the base of the cone [Teide]. It was possible to go higher via two trails to the edge of the crater from where you could see the whole of the island. We were content to climb up through the lava rock, with much heavy breathing, to the viewing point a short way above from where we were standing.

The view was awesome; the thoughts of what nature could do *and* over many years was overwhelming and humbling food for thought. You realize how insignificant we individual humans are in the grander scheme of things. Some very early visitors were on their way down. Joan and Rob had advised us that we would need a warm jumper or jacket due to the height. In fact, all the information advises of the need for a jumper. These hardy souls told us that it was freezing. They were only in thin tops and shorts having ignored the advice. Well, it was so hot down by the sea.

After getting someone nearby to take a photo of the four of us as we sat on top of the world with a blanket of fluffy white clouds below us, we gingerly made our way down. Many coach parties were by now arriving at the cable car station where the tourists were forced to form a long queue in the searing June heat.

In the coolness of the early evening, we decided to visit **Los Gigantes,** a little further south on this west coast. This was our first visit to see these giant rocks which seem to march into the sea. The setting sun cast a wonderful display of light as it beamed down through the clouds. Many boats were moored up in the harbour while waterside bars and cafés were ready for another evening of fun, food, and laughter.

Our menfolk were to be seen peering down into the water catching sight of quite large fish swimming there without a care.

'Lots of big fish,' Allen is heard to comment. 'Estimated length eighteen to twenty-four inches.' This was pre-metric time.

For myself, I was so excited, I had to capture everything. We had only had the camcorder for less than twelve months. I had won it in a manufacturer's product knowledge competition where you had to make a product-related film. (I was working in electrical sales.) It came just in time for Allen's fiftieth birthday but he soon decided that he preferred his stills camera. I for my part fell in love with the camcorder, resulting in many hours of filming on increasingly common 'adventures' followed by more hours of editing. Firstly, via TV onto VHS tapes before progressing to digital tapes and computer software.

Now, we spent some time at a waterside bar with the dramatic backdrop of the giant cliffs rising out of the sea while the sun shed its last rays, shooting into the sky with glorious colour.

Watching the video as I write this, it was fun to see how, after dinner in the hotel, the styles of dancing have changed. What hasn't changed however, is how many couples enjoy more formal ballroom dancing.

Tonight's entertainment was a troupe of scantily clad African dancers, with their steel drums, tribal headdresses, and fast and furious tribal music. The lady dancers were also scantily clad but wore grass skirts. It was a good show of very acrobatic, tribal dancing all round. There was the usual act of walking under a very low off-the-floor pole. Eager members of the audience needed little encouragement to try their skill. Men showed off their prowess and agility in dancing under the low pole without knocking the pole off the supports. Fire eating skills rounded off this energetic act.

Afterwards, they were happy to have a photo taken with guests.

Day 4 tour.

Today's programme would take us along the north coast to **Icod de los Vinos** and **La Orotava.**

Icod de los Vinos is an old town now famous for the three-thousand-year old Dragon Tree. Rising high into the sky, it widens out at the top as its branches spread out above a mass of old branches twisted together to form the trunk. A clump of spiky leaves sprouts from the end of each branch.

The resort is small but a visit almost compulsory in order to see the 'Drago' or Dragon Tree. Outside, among an array of roses and white agapanthus flowers, a man showed off his parrots, insisting with gestures that I didn't film him. Part of his work and living, my husband informed me, was to have photos taken with visitors and his parrots for money.

As we were here on an independent visit we just stopped briefly, not exploring the town. Also, not realising how much there was to see and experience. On a later visit we did learn and see more under the eyes of a guide.

Driving on along the north coast, we turned inland through the **Orotava Valley** to the town of **Orotava** that is famous for its houses with typical Canarian balconies and **La Casa de los Balcones** which is now a Visitor Centre.

Overlooking the narrow streets, many of the houses have balconies that are typical of the island. The wooden balconies are distinctive with their sloping roofs. The fifteenth century Casa de los Balcones is now a Casa Turista or Tourist Centre. It also has crafts of many kinds on display.

Entering the imposing stone archway with a balcony above and many others on the windows of the white walls, we passed a wall display of framed pictures.

'The balconies of the houses are typical of the Canary Islands,' I recorded into the camcorder.

'They appear to be stuck onto the wall as a post on each corner of wooden balcony supports an angled tiled roof.'

Inside, we found a colourful display of all kinds of lace, embroidery, and 'cut work' made into all manner of articles to tempt the visitor. Not only the usual tablecloths and napkins but lace-edged fans and lace-edged flamenco dresses with many frills and flounces. Capturing our eye was a very old-fashioned till where you pressed the correct buttons to ring up the price and open the till drawer. Its brass work shone in a well-polished way.

On show, were many wicker baskets. A man sat among them, demonstrating his skills in how they were made. The walls of the whole courtyard were covered from top to bottom in a wonderful display of the skills of the craft workers. Above, many balconies surrounded the walls, with windows thrown open to catch the coolness of the interior. Palm trees which rose high into the sky gave more shade. The fronts of the balconies were ornate with wooden carvings.

A display of work-in-progress caught my eye. It was drawn thread work with intricate patterns emerging from the straight threads. Some parts were so elaborate and intricate as to appear like lace made by using bobbins.

'We will see what we can spend our money on now.' I am heard to inform my husband.

Outside, we refreshed ourselves in the tea rooms before going back inside where a lady dressed in Canarian costume of white blouse and colourful waistcoat and skirt was back at her station. Working on a long table runner, she drew the threads into various patterns as she knotted stitches around them.

And then we saw a masterpiece. A sand drawing of a Madonna and Child. The artist used many shades and colours of sand to form his picture as he carefully trickled a few grains at a time through his hand to apply them to the floor. He was working off a picture in a book. It was remarkable.

In another corner, a cigar-maker arranged large, pliable, tobacco leaves on a block, packed tobacco into a dip at one end and, bringing forward a handle, rolled the contents forward to form a cigar which he placed to one side ready for a final finish of cellophane and packing for despatch.

We did extend the car hire for another day when my husband took the wheel and both couples went their own way for a day to do 'their own thing' on this short holiday in the warm sunshine of Tenerife, but soon, all too soon, with a lingering look from the balcony at this beautiful island and sparkling sea, it was time to pack up and go. With one last look at the island as the plane soared into the sky, we knew that we would have to return.

When my special Valentine birthday came along a few years later there was only one place to go. Tenerife.

Winter sunshine in Los Cristianos.

When I reached the milestone of fifty years, we celebrated with a wonderful holiday in Tenerife as sunshine was more or less guaranteed in the Canary Islands. Coming to land, despite heavy cloud I filmed what I could of the approach to the island through the window of the plane regardless.

We treated ourselves to a stay at the Hotel Arona Gran, situated at the far end of the town which was not as developed as it later became. We continued with this tradition for some years as my birthday fell in February and we longed to escape the chills and damp of the UK.

Our hotel was far more luxurious than we had every thought we would be able to experience. The long lounge area with its many relaxing chairs, sofas, and a profusion of plants cascading from the balconies above, which led to the rooms, gave a quiet, peaceful, and cool area in which to relax.

Listening to music in the piano bar was a pleasant way to enjoy a pre-dinner cocktail. The dining room with a varied buffet and show cooking was excellent as was the after-dinner entertainment in the bar lounge which came later in the evening.

Spending many relaxing hours by the excellent pool of the hotel which overlooked the sea and promenade; strolling along the sea front into the town to browse in the embroidery and jeweller's shops, sometimes to buy; exploring the harbour area; all made for a perfect holiday.

******

Los Cristianos as we know it today has expanded from the old fishing village of yesteryear into the thriving holiday resort that it is today. Although the promenade is flat, the nature of the volcanic terrain means that the town is in a slightly elevated position rising above the sea with many steps to reach the higher levels. From the hotel, we could either take the main road with a long slope upwards and outwards towards the livelier side of town and turn towards the centre of town up a very steep slope or by the steps. The other way and our favourite was to meander along the flat promenade and the seafront, passing other hotels, to the old part and the harbour. As the land rose, there were short flights of steps plus a slight ramp for mobility scooters of which I might add, there were many with the other half of the couple sometimes hitching a ride on the back.

We loved to head out along the sea wall to look at the boats and the day-to-day business of the fishermen. From here we could either carry on along the new beach with its golden sand (imported from the Sahara Desert) which joins Los Cristianos with Playa de las Americas or turn into town with its many cafes, restaurants, embroidery shops, jeweller's shops, leather, and other craft shops along the long main street that led to the Plaza and the church in the centre of town. The walk back to our hotel was a very steep downhill and a pleasant walk.

One year we whiled away some time by browsing in one of the leather shops. Undeterred by my husband's insistence that he was not going to buy anything, the friendly shopkeeper eventually persuaded him. Although Allen's manner of disinterest was genuine, the shopkeeper took this as a bargaining ploy. In either case, it worked as we ended up with a very good outcome.

I have said that my birthday fell in February and that we chose to come away around this time. To this end, I did not receive a present on my birthday if we were still at home but saved the present buying for when we reached Los Cristianos where we could browse in the jeweller's shops for earrings or a watch etc. What a nice way to spend a holiday.

******

With our horizons rapidly expanding, we returned the following year to the Arona Gran. We thought that we would have to abandon our plans as, sitting in the pub the evening before the flight enjoying a meal (no food in the house) we exclaimed at the pretty snowflakes which had started to come down.

The following morning Allen, clad in boots and jacket, had to dig the car out of the snow at home. Eventually reaching Manchester Airport, we found the flight delayed while machines sprayed de-icing fluid over our plane. What a relief when we boarded and had clearance for take-off. All expectation, we headed for the sunshine and Los Cristianos.

Masca Valley.

During this time of our escape to the sun, we had also started to meet up in Tenerife with our daughter's parents-in-law, Bob and Terri, who had an apartment on the island at the same time as we were there. Becoming firm friends over recent years, we usually enjoyed a day out on their top floor apartment balcony with extensive views high above the rooftops across to the sea below with a backdrop of mountains behind. Over the years, we visited the Casino in Las Americas where we ladies had fun with our little pot of 'chips' as our menfolk waited indulgently for us to lose them all. On *this* occasion, it *was* actually the day of my birthday – a point noted by the security man as he checked my passport before entry to the Casino.

Sometimes, we strolled in the Puerto Colon area at the Torviscas end of Las Americas where palm trees, plants, and succulents lent an elegant air as you walked along the promenade in the sunshine listening to a singer. At almost six o'clock the temperature was *down* to twenty-five degrees.

One year [1999], we hired a driver to take us around as neither of the men wanted to drive a hire car.

We had settled on the **Masca Valley** and the village of Masca on the north-west of the island. It was quite difficult to get to as the village was accessed down the unforgiving steep, winding, mountain switchback roads. The winding road to Masca had, as usual, the backdrop of Teide which, this year, was well covered in snow. A wall protected us from the sheer drop down the mountainside. Stopping briefly at a viewing point we drank in the view of this verdant part of the island with the contrast of black, jagged mountains towering over the valley. Verdant as there is more rain in the north to feed the plants. Our driver took this brief stop to discuss the route to the village down below.

'If you live down there, that is Masca, or part of Masca,' he explained haltingly, a little unsure.

The road snaked through and around the mountains. High peaks swept down either side to form a 'V' shape. There was a lot of vegetation both on the road level and on the lower slopes.

'Oh, dear. That bus is stuck. It's got to back up to get around that corner.' I was sympathetic.

The views were incredible. I constantly reflect in awe, 'How clever is God.' No human being could possibly create the unending varied landscape and vista which changes at every twist and turn in every corner of the world. The scenery here was impressive; the winding road swept in twists and turns as it wound around the mountain and deep into the valley. It was very wild while the sky was blue with little cloud.

The sun was by now getting hot as it rose in the sky. Being winter the days were shorter therefore the sun reached its peak later in the morning. The roads here were recent as previously there was only a footpath or tracks that the mules use. As you can imagine, the construction of roads opened-up access to the valley for visitors.

There were many stopping places for taking in the view and photos. The road was now busy with a group of trucks full of jolly young men singing their hearts out. They had to pass another one which had stopped at a bend in the mountain road to allow them to pass. Singing lustily, they continued down the hillside.

Driving on, 'That's a house down there.'

Surprisingly, massive electricity pylons reared up the mountainside from the deep valley below. There were also modern street lights to light up the edge of the road.

Finding a stopping place and parking up we carefully made our way to a steep cobbled path.

'We are now in Masca and I think that we are going to find something to eat,' I said for the camera.

The rough road led us steeply down the hillside (like mountain goats we were), past a telephone booth – a sign of habitation – palm trees, and all kinds of other trees, vegetation, and flowering plants at either side of the path. The sheer mountainside rose before us in the sunshine.

After refreshing ourselves with coffee, while our driver caught his breath after the steep descent, we took the opportunity to visit the Ceramic de Masca. The Ceramic Shop had the usual array of goods to tempt the visitor. What a pity that luggage restrictions prevented me from indulging in a spate of spending on the enticing range of pottery on offer.

Deep in the fertile valley, where the land formed a green carpet before us, we could see that farmers were busy with their crops. The flowers were as beautiful as the landscaped views as they swept across the valley to the sea. Our driver was a Scotsman who lived on the island. He was very informative and allowed us many opportunities for photo shoots on this special day out where ribbons of road around the terraced land wound through the mountains. The dramatic rock formations appeared to be like walls rearing up into the sky to protect those in the valley below.

The steep road further into the valley twists and turns through **Macizo de Teno Massif** until it reaches **Buenavista del Norte** on the north-westerly tip of the island and the sea. It would be a brave person who ventured down there, I thought with a little shiver, but wondered how it would be on our recently purchased Gold Wing motorbike. Shh.

Garachico.

However back to reality now and the main road to the fishing village of Garachico on the north-west coast near **Icod de los Vinos**. We had visited there some years previously you will recall, on our first visit to Tenerife when other friends introduced us to the island. As we had seen something of the island on this first visit, we had some idea of where the driver could take us for lunch. Now *we* in turn could show our family friends something of the island as we directed our driver where to go next.

Turning northwards we went over the mountain to the fishing village of Garachico on the north coast where we had heard about a good place to eat at on the sea front. The sea still battered the sea wall so we were a bit doubtful as to its suitability. A crane was attached to a small fishing boat as the fisherman gathered his equipment ready for his boat to be hauled up out of the sea and over the sea wall to dry land.

'Oh, he is actually coming up.' Allen pointed out.

'It is fascinating,' I was awed. 'It is one way of getting out of there.'

There was quite a breeze; water crashed over the sea wall noisily as we strolled along the sea front. Behind us the mountain rose, a sheer wall of rock where the road snaked up and over it. White-walled shops had their awnings out in protection against the fierce sun; cars went about their business, probably home for lunch as it was almost siesta time.

After examining the old castle/fort of San Miguel on the promenade, we settled down for lunch at the harbour side restaurant, inviting our driver to eat at our expense (we think that he expected it). It was a hot day and we were glad of the sea air and the shady umbrellas as we enjoyed a lovely lunch while observing what was going on in the sea.

Watching in relaxed pleasure as the high strong breakers crashed into the sea wall, our gaze took us again across the road to the mountain high above along which the road over its top ran. All you could see was a white snake along the mountainside where the road climbed its way ever upwards to the main highway above. We were not to know that, sometime in the future, we would ride along this road on a scooter. Oh, ignorance is bliss.

'We are going to make our way to **Orotava** and the House of Balconies.'

I recorded our discussion for the camera. This was where the fun began.

Orotava Valley.

We wanted to show Bob and Terri the village of La Orotava and La Casa de Los Balcones or House of Balconies more eastwards and inland from **Puerto de la Cruz.** The driver did not seem to know of this little gem but I pulled out the maps and we persuaded him that *we* would direct *him*. A local? He wasn't a native of Tenerife but a Scotsman living on the island.

Off we set and eventually, following signposts and memory we arrived in the village. The traditional houses in this area were built around a courtyard and had balconies on the house walls within the courtyard as well as outside. La Casa de Los Balcones was an excellent example of a Canarian House; it had been turned into a Museum and Craft Workshop.

The display of Crafts and Workmanship – mainly lace and woven goods – was as profuse and varied as on our earlier visit and still with many examples of embroidery to tempt you. Being hand-made, the price reflects the skills involved in the creation of the article. I love the various types of embroidery and lace available in the islands, so much so that one year my husband made me promise not to buy any more. (On a mental re-cap, we have embroidery and lace from Bruges, Venice, Cyprus, Sorrento, Tenerife, Madeira and more. All different.) It is worth noting that an affordable gift is a handkerchief which has a little lace on a corner.

The huge runner of drawn thread work that I talked about earlier was complete on this visit. Or was it another one? There was also a display of how a traditional wine press would have worked, artefacts and life-sized figures in traditional dress. The waterwheel among the plants threw water into a pipe whereupon it tipped over and emptied back into the container.

Another fountain tinkled as water cascaded down various bowls. It all added to the cool and inviting ambience.

As I recounted earlier on our first visit, another surprising skill was 'sand painting' where the artist creates, on the floor, a picture with different colours of sand. The sand artist was still there; his skill was astounding to witness as he directed grains of sand onto the floor to complete his 'painting'. Bob and Terri found this amazing and what an end to a lovely day. We were also pleased to have been able to show our friends another aspect of the island, away from the Playas of the south coast.

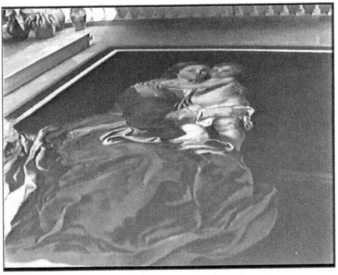

SAND PAINTING AT LA CASA DE LOS BALCONES.
OROTAVA VALLEY TENERIFE

Later, on our balcony at the hotel, we could see a huge white [gas filled?] balloon hanging over the blue sea behind the high-rise hotels of Los Cristianos and the harbour. Below, hanging from it was a basket. Allen was trying to focus with the camcorder on all the building work which was going on behind the hotel. The noise of machinery was testament to this.

In the distance, Mount Teide and snow-covered slopes dominated the scene. Today, some years later, I noticed from maps on the Internet, that far from our hotel being on the edge of development in this lovely corner of Los Cristianos with nothing between our hotel and the mountain at the side, there is much development and another hotel. But at the time all *that* was in the future. For now, I found that, unbeknown to me, climbing *that* mountain was on someone's agenda.

Exploring the Adeje area.

We started off 2003, with another trip to Tenerife, staying this time in the Fañabe area north of Playa de las Americas. This stretch of coast a little further north was now being developed into a more upmarket tourist destination to cater for more discerning clients of other nationalities. The area boundaries had been re-defined at this point with the rivers or Ribeira being the separation marker. The area below the mountain village of Arona was now named Arona. The area below the mountain village of Adeje was named Adeje with Las Americas in the middle. The Costa Adeje area took in Fañabe, Torviscas, and Puerto Colon and the marina. Our hotels in Fañabe were out of this world and to my joy, quite near clothes shops where I could buy floaty, cool dresses.

The coast along this stretch became rockier as we headed toward the newly developed hotel and beach area. The sea crashed and banged, at time shooting through holes in the rocks sending spray high into the air. We loved to stand and watch this exhilarating force of nature. The main hotel here was El Duque which not only came down to the beach but was often set out for fine dining on the beach. With silver service, of course; it was a very upmarket hotel.

We contented ourselves with the simple enjoyment of watching the world go by and buying ice-cream in the nearby beach kiosk. Wandering away from the sea, we found many new apartment blocks and very smart shops. It was interesting to see over the course of a couple of years how the area had grown.

A visit to Tenerife would not be complete (for me) without a little bit of retail therapy. The truth was that I loved the fashions and fabrics of the beautiful garments which are made for a hot climate and were also suitable for the few very hot days that we experienced in the UK. Negotiating the steep path to the small shopping centre quite near to the Bahia Princess, I fell for two lovely outfits. One was a floaty dress in black with a white pattern with a matching floaty loose coat. It would be perfect to wear for meetings etc. in work on hot days in summer. The other was a loose dress with a double layer of two shades of turquoise/sea blue. This was matched by a floaty coat to match. At the bottom edge of both dress and coat were huge embroidered fronds of leaves.

When I put it on that night for dinner, I commented that it really was nice enough to wear at a wedding. I didn't speak too soon as, a few weeks after arriving home, our son telephoned to announce that 'they had set a date' for their wedding later that year. This sea blue outfit would be perfect. One of our daughters also rang during this call to say that she was engaged and would be getting married, as it turned out a month before the other one.

'No. You can't.' I protested firmly, 'I will have a nervous breakdown. You will have to delay a couple of months.'

They did. And I did wear the floaty dress to our son's wedding later that year.

Climbing a mountain.

The morning dawned when I was to trek over a mountain as later in our holiday my husband insisted that we go for a walk; the exercise 'would do me good'.

Even today, many years later, when I say refer to the mountain, Allen scoffs,

'It wasn't a mountain; it was only a little hill.'

Well, Mount Cumplida at one hundred and forty-one metres (four hundred and sixty-five feet) was high enough for me and, more to the point, involved sensible shoes. Not expecting a mountaineering adventure, I wasn't sure that I had packed any as I don't do 'sensible'. Low-heeled mules are as far as I go in the 'sensible' stakes. Often gold colour or beige. And zig-zagging like a mountain goat? Agile I am **not**.

Leaving behind my sunbed, the sound of the sea in front of me, and the assignment that I had brought with me (I was studying for an Honours Degree in Education), we set off to trek over the mountain at Los Cristianos taking with us our water, sandwiches in case we couldn't find food, and sunhats.

Up we trekked along the rocky and unmarked path as Los Cristianos and our hotel fell far below us. The view, as my husband 'encouraged' me along this winding, very narrow, stony path up the side of the mountain, unfolded in front of us to include the town of Los Cristianos and beyond. As I said earlier, then there was little development beyond our hotel, a situation which was to change judging from all the marking out we could see.

Allen was filming the view down to the coast. He was doing this for my safety so that I would not overbalance in my eagerness not to miss anything.

'I don't know if I got all that, because I could have just pushed the wrong button.'

He was filming the rock formation and water channels (an engineer to the last).

'It is there on the bottom left. You have to get the habit.' I shared my knowledge.

'It is the time as well. It is the time ticking by that I am looking at,' he explained.

As we climbed, we could see our hotel down below and the other side of the outcrop east of Los Cristianos where paragliders take off over the sea. It is lovely to be 'up there' and see the coastline spread out below; specially to see Mount Teide far away dominating the island. The landscape was barren and desolate; turning to look across and down to the other side a lone bus came into view. At least there was some life here somewhere and we were not completely alone.

Panning the camcorder over the flat area as we reached the top, I commented,

'This is the new plantation, isn't it?'

'The new growing area,' Allen corrected.

The new growing areas were under plastic. They were massive structures covering large, square areas of land which stretched as far as the eye could see. Now walking on the flat land among the growing areas one or two walkers and a vehicle passed us by. Civilization?

Resting to eat our sandwiches and reflecting on our adventure so far, we idly watched the aeroplanes coming to land at the nearby airport in the south. This was a Friday and a busy day with arrivals and departures every ten minutes or so.

'We have come over the mountain and are looking ahead to Las Galletas.'

I continued to talk into the camcorder as I swung it around. There wasn't a soul about. The small party that had passed us were long gone. On their merry way.

'There's a bus,' I exclaimed in relief at signs of civilization.

Laughingly, Allen joked,' There's a bus, golly gosh, a bus.'

In the distance, we could see slow-moving traffic on a lone road that we later learned started from the development of Palm Mar on the coast on to Guaza and then to meet the road back to Los Cristianos.

Walking on, we came upon a sign.

'Monumento Natural.'

'Montaña de Guaza.'

At *430 metres (1400 ft.)* the sign also told us that we were in a Natural Protected Space.

'Sale Usted de un Espacio.'

'Natural Protegido.'

'Buen Viaje. (Good Journey.)'

On entering the National Park there was not a soul in sight and if we had had an accident, who would have helped us? We do take some chances don't we but, nothing ventured, nothing gained and I had Allen to look after me. Although on reflection, as he doesn't speak a word of Spanish I don't know how he could have helped.

'A bit of cacti there.' I focused on a large batch of cactus plants nestling among the stones.

'Now, tell me again about those water channels.' They were a feature of the landscape here.

'What about them? They are made from lava rock, they are about one metre long with chunks, all chiselled out for the water and then joined together with cement. From a distance, it looks like breeze block.'

Allen was a fount of knowledge. A group of early walkers passed us on their way up.

'And there is Teide,' I observed, 'with cloud just going over the top of it.'

Allen cracked one of his dreadful jokes. Aye. A tidy sight, isn't it?' Groan. Chuckle.

'No giggling.'

'Why?'

'The camera shakes.'

'There is a vehicle coming past.' A four-wheel drive vehicle passed us. From whence he had come I know not.

'My word. Civilization,' I continued.

Looking northwards to a line in the distance, I observed,

That's the motorway over there, isn't it?'

I pointed in the direction that I was talking about. Signs of habitation in this desolate area backed by rising mountains were welcome as you can imagine.

Walking through the Banana Plantations, a bed of bananas caused us to agree that they didn't look very well looked after. There were 'hands' or huge bunches of green bananas ripening in the sun among the banana leaves. Although there were water pipes, Allen thought that, 'someone had turned them on and turned them off.'

One clump or 'hand' was an unripen green. How bananas grow is an education as they do not grow how you imagine them to – hanging down.

'As they grow they turn, upwards don't they?'

(We had learned this in Madeira, that they don't start off as they finish.) Instead we could see that they grow and turn upwards along the trunk.

Allen continued remarking about the stems on the plant.

'There is the old one, the new one beside it, and a tiddly little new one for next year.'

(There was the old trunk, the current one with fruit and a new one growing at the side ready for next year.)

'Oh, yes.' I was all wonder at this discovery. Or at least a reminder of an earlier discovery which must have left my brain's internal hard drive.

We came to Las Galletas on the coast which was very dramatic and rugged. This was the other side of Los Cristianos. The sea crashed onto the rocky shore. The boats, bobbing in the harbour, had their sails wrapped up.

'We have walked, and walked, ("and walked," Allen interrupted) until we came to Ten-Bel near the airport.'

'Got ten bells,' said the joker.'

'We've *not* got ten bells; well you might have ten bells. We are now in Costa Silencio.' The above banter is from being long-time married.

Ten-Bel with modern holiday apartments and shops is a purpose-built area of Costa Silencio on the very south of the island. Being usually very hot it is a magnet for sun-lovers. We thought initially, that we would not like to stay here as there was no character, much preferring Los Cristianos with its old town, traditional shops, and harbour but people come here to soak up the sun by their pools and it is probably good for children. In Costa Silencio, proper made-up roads lined with palm trees and pavements, street lights, beautiful buildings with arched windows, and cars, greeted us. Wow. And a zebra crossing and roundabout. Another world.

'It is quite near the airport here and that it why it is quite noisy with the aeroplanes.' *(Writing this transcript now, I realized that I had forgotten this small point when I booked our forthcoming 'field trip' for 2017. Oops. I will let you know if we did find it noisy with aeroplanes.)*

Allen commented that there was, 'A beautiful view of Mount Teide.'

'With the snow on top for a cap.' I responded.

I continued filming, 'We are going to go down the street, find something to eat, and then get on the bus to go back to our hotel.'

We were still a little hungry after eating our earlier sandwiches. I continued panning the camcorder around.

'There again is Mount Teide with his head in the clouds.'

The telephoto lens was amazing, especially added to the excellent zoom on the camcorder.

'In the distance is Ten-Bel from where we have just come and we are back in Las Galletas [on the coast].'

The beach below the rocky coast was stony; the new development here [Las Galletas] bordered the sun-facing seashore, on this very southerly part of the island. *(Perhaps I won't notice the aeroplanes when we come next year.)* As usual, I am filming my feet as the camcorder, still on 'record', swung from my shoulder as we walked.

I can confirm that I was *not* wearing sensible shoes but low-heeled mules with a good covering of the foot.

That is about as sensible as it gets with me. I think that they were a gold colour.

Later, standing on a promenade lined with palm trees I commented,

'Los Cristianos is on the other side of that bay.'

And then I took a shot of the boats in the harbour; all kinds of boats from small ones to sleek launches; fishing boats pulled out of the water; with the mountain that we had just walked over behind us as a backdrop.

'It is not a mountain,' I can hear Allen saying.

With one last look, I reluctantly (or was it eagerly) queried,

'We will now go back to Los Cristianos shall we?'

'Yes.'

And with that, we walked to the bus stop to catch the bus for the short journey along the main road to Los Cristianos.

We spent the rest of our stay, enjoying the wonderful facilities of our hotel, strolling into the town, and soaking up the relaxing sound of the sea. As I filmed from our balcony the evening sights over the harbour – the lights and boats – a cruise ship from the Fred Olsen line with lights blazing from the towering decks and portholes sailed majestically and smoothly into its berth for the night. Such a romantic and enticing scene.

Many sunbeds at the hotel were reserved with towels each morning. We tried and tried but in the end, we could not resist and had to succumb. We did it. We came down early and bagged our sunbeds. Then after breakfast, Allen would get the mattresses and towels. On our last day, we had a late flight and decided to spend the morning, before check-out, by the pool. With one last look around the terraces, I captured once again the beauty and tranquility that surrounded us.

'And so, we come to the end of *this* Atlantic Adventure. (The Azores and Madeira that I chatted about earlier, had preceded this visit.) It has been a fantastic couple of months. We are leaving the Arona Gran – until next time.'

We were in fact, to visit again the following year before visiting other islands that I have recounted in our expanded Atlantic Adventure. Our next visits to Tenerife were to the Fañabe area and two more hotels in the Torviscas area which are all part of the Costa Adeje.

To Mount Teide on a scooter.

My husband, having withdrawal symptoms at not being on the Gold Wing motorbike, thought that he would pretend and rent a *scooter*. Strolling through the resort, we saw a scooter hire place. Making a bee-line for this we looked at the scooters outside, chatted with the receptionist and arranged to collect one the following day.

Now, you must realize that climbing on the back of a little 100cc scooter was a different ball game to the luxury of the 'Queen' seat which was my usual perch on our Gold Wing 1500cc motorbike. Hoping with trepidation and a slight shudder that they were clean, we put on the provided helmets and climbed aboard. Allen fired up the engine, and off we set with only a little wobble until we got the hang of it. Remembering that we were to drive on the right and following the signposts out of town we slowly joined the noisy bustle of traffic and hit the main road to go up Mount Teide. I say 'we' but it was Allen who was in the driving seat. I was simply clinging on to the passenger seat with the hand-holds provided. That is, if you can call the small space behind the rider a seat.

It was a glorious day with the sun rising in a blue sky. The journey snaking up through pine forests was uneventful on the windy and winding roads. Climbing higher up the southern slopes, my husband was concerned at the alarming rate in which the fuel gauge dropped. Halfway up, we stopped for a cooling drink in a mountain village whereupon my mobile phone rang, disturbing other people. Surprise, surprise, it was one of my learners/students trying to discuss a point in her learning programme. I quickly explained that I was not in the office [an understatement], was on leave and would contact her on my return. Such dedication but at least I answered.

Continuing ever upwards through the changing scenery of verdant slopes which gave way to a more barren lava rock we eventually came to the cable car station and restaurant.

Parking up, we removed our helmets and drank in the view. For posterity, I took a photo of Allen with his 'substitute' motorbike. I jest but truly, riding on a motorbike up a mountain is the best way to absorb the scenery as you are 'at one' with the world and it is a quite different experience to driving up in a car.

In the restaurant with its huge wide windows, we found a window seat from where we could admire the views of this fairly barren volcanic landscape. You will remember that we had been up to the top of the mountain on the cable car on our first visit and decided not to do so again, mainly as we were nervous of leaving the hire scooter unattended. The journey up to this highest mountain in Spain on a little scooter with a limited petrol tank, had used up quite a lot of petrol; we had but a drop left for the journey down.

'The fuel gauge is showing *empty*,' came a concerned and slightly panicky voice in front of me as we sailed down the northern side of the mountain.

'Well, if we run out we will just have to coast down.' I was all practicality.

The northern slopes of Mount Teide are very green, not least as this is where most of the rain falls. Twisting and turning with many gear changes as we followed bend after bend, we could drink in the stupendous views of the lush Orotava Valley. At one point, about halfway down the mountain, we came upon two young lads. Thankfully, we stopped and with sign language and gesturing to the petrol tank we asked how far to the petrol station.

'One kilometre.'

With smiles and a thank you/gracias, we continued our way, eyes peeled for the promised fuel stop. Well, on and on we went but no fuel.

'I think he meant one kilometre straight down the mountainside,' Allen commented. 'It is a very long one kilometre.'

He really was getting, not just concerned, but desperate, not being sure how much fuel the reserve tank had left. Here we were, again 'just us two' riding down a mountainside with barely a soul in sight. We hadn't stopped to think of the consequences if anything had happened to us. But if you do that too much you would never do anything, would you?

As luck, would have it we eventually and just in time found the petrol station in the Orotava Valley where we filled the fuel tank and headed towards the main coast road.

Garachico.

Riding along the northern coast we came upon Garachico, the fishing village on the north-west coast. Stopping to look around and get our bearings, we recalled that we had visited this fishing village twice before with friends on previous visits. To head south and get back to Adeje we had to go over the mountain. Another mountain. The signposts indicated that we turn left away from the sea. This road rose steeply onto the high road; it snaked up the mountainside with only a low white wall between us and the sheer drop into the sea below.

The view as I looked down from my perch behind Allen was out of this world. I could see the whole of the coastline with the sea crashing on the rocks below. (In 2007, we were to visit again and reflect how we had made the journey on a little scooter. No, we hadn't been mad – just grabbing all the experiences we could while we could).

The northern coast had been a chilly contrast from the sun on Mount Teide. Clearing the mountain, we were glad to turn southwards, past the signs for San Francisco, Santiago del Teide, and through the Banana Plantations as the sun warmed us. The contrast really was surprising; it was as if we were in two different countries.

Reaching the coast and our very plush hotel, the Bahia Princess, where smart cars populate the garage, the security guard there was very dubious of letting us park up our little scooter. He snootily and suspiciously looked us up and down as if we were a bad smell, ready to turn us away. This little scooter did not really fit the image of the hotel and clientele. Even when we showed him our room card, he was reluctant to let us in but, the universal impact of Gold Wing motorbikes came to the rescue. When we pointed to our GWOCGB logos on our fleeces, a look of marked respect came into his eyes, 'Aahhh! Goldwing!' and he understood. Parking up was no longer a problem as he directed us to the garages – quite respectfully I might add.

A birthday treat – a helicopter ride.

Another year. Another big birthday. Again, staying at another 'Princess' Hotel in the Fañabe area of what is now known as Costa Adeje. This time, the elegant and stylish Guayarmina Princess. As I said earlier, this area has been massively developed as a separate area from Las Americas with a range of very upmarket hotels, apartments, and shops. For my birthday treat I was keen to have a helicopter ride as I thought that it would be wonderful to see the area from the sky. Allen was dubious at the cost.

'But you had a CB radio for the Gold Wing for your big birthday, I protested. There was no argument that could move me. 'All I want is a little helicopter ride. Not a helicopter.' I was firm.

Suffice to say that the trip was booked and we made our way on the appointed day to the helipad location. Unfortunately, there was much low cloud but my excitement did not abate. I must say that you do need to be agile to climb into a helicopter. The distance between ground and cockpit was quite steep. Another couple on the trip settled for going in the rear seat while I, once I had heaved myself aided by a big push from behind into the cockpit, sat beside the pilot.

After following all his pre-flight checks, he took off towards Los Gigantes. As I said, it was quite cloudy but nevertheless there much to see. The view from above, with the coastline and mountains laid out before us was stupendous. Leaving the south behind, we could see how fertile was the northern side of the island. The pilot pointed out the major landmarks before turning around to skim over the coast and back to base.

BIRTHDAY TREAT – NOT THE ACTUAL HELICOPTER.

Puerto Santiago, Tenerife, March 2007.

We continued our increasing love affair with Saga destinations and the sunshine islands with yet another visit to Tenerife. We were now using the increasingly wide variety of Saga Holidays more and more. Not least because of the excursions to the interior which were often included. In addition, with changing needs and limitations, we found that Saga Holidays ticked all the boxes such as included insurance, porterage of luggage, advance location information about the terrain, and possible difficulties with mobility considerations on excursions or hotel location.

Due to the unsettled weather, which we had experienced the previous two years in the Canary Islands, we decided to go out a little later than normal.

Wishing to take advantage of the 'all-inclusive' offers of Saga Holidays, we had to choose a different location to one that we would have preferred.

Puerto Santiago is a little further north on the west coast than Adeje and near Los Gigantes where the sheer cliffs plunge down into the sea. The town itself was above the rocky coast with a long coast road snaking along between the hotels, shops, and apartments on one side and the sea and beaches on the other. We had ridden around this town a few years previously when we had hired a scooter and knew it to be quite hilly in places. The hotel however was in a level location but it was a steep slope down to the sea in some places. Usually we kept on the high road which led straight into the town.

One reason also, for choosing this location was the full day included trip to the Taganana Valley which is in the most north-eastern peninsula of the island. The Taganana Valley and its lush green forests and valleys, was the only part of the island we hadn't seen in twelve years of wintering in Tenerife. This, sold it to us.

Prior to our leaving date, Saga had telephoned to say that at the hotel in Puerto Santiago, some building work was going on next door and that we could cancel if we wished. Being assured that Saga rooms were away from the building work we decided to go ahead as we would be out of the hotel during the day.

It was a good choice and, with many clients cancelling it wasn't feasible for the hotel to open a day long bar. Instead, the hotel set up a bar in an alcove off a patio. This bar had a barrel of beer on tap along with soft drinks. There was also an amazing selection of wines, spirits, and liqueurs such as we had never seen before; I think that there was one of almost everything produced.

And it was self-service. It was so pleasant to sit in the sun with a good book and a glass of something cold.

'Just fill me up darling,' one or the other would gently prompt as we turned a page in the book that we were reading.

Another visit to Garachico and Icod de los Vinos.

Waking early in the morning of this 'all-inclusive' excursion, I bounded onto the balcony as usual to soak up the morning senses and smells as the town came to life after a busy evening. The outline of the island of La Gomera twenty-four miles away was clearly visible from where I was standing, as a long grey shape.

'The sun is just rising and it is coming over the mountains behind us; it is just shining on the island. The clouds are a bit thin, lying over the top of the island which I believe is always in cloud,' I recorded.

Later in the day, from the mountain road that we were travelling on in the north-west of Tenerife, we had a good view of Garachico spread out as it was below us with the mound of the rock of Garachico in the sea. (This is the road that we rode up we on the hire scooter in 2003. Golly gosh.)

The mountainsides were very green; a contrast to the blue sea and huddle of red roofs of buildings below. Electricity pylons marched down the steep slopes. Zooming in on the camcorder, I could clearly see the low, white wall which prevented road users from crashing over the edge of the road into the sea below. Another 'wow'.

Moving on through pine forests, we were soon in **Icod** where we were to visit the famous Dragon Tree – El Drago, the Market, Parish Church, and an old wine press.

EL DRAGO – DRAGON TREE.

'We are now in Icod de los Vinos and this is the famous Dragon Tree. The church bell is ringing behind me. A pleasant sound. When we first came all those years ago, we were able to walk around the tree but now they have built a wall around it.'

'I think to preserve it from the fumes off cars etc. and now, you have to pay to go in [the Parque del Drago].'

With all the flagpoles and flags fluttering in the breeze, it certainly made a tourist feature while preserving the ancient tree.

Ladies standing behind nearby tables filled with craft goods were industrially busy with weaving baskets, dishes and other items which lent themselves to the art of weaving.

Moving down the street, we came upon the ancient church of San Marcos. The entrance fee was only €1 Euro and decided to take advantage of an opportunity to look inside, finding to be a very sturdy church. The wide, circular pillars and archways framing the paintings on the walls blended the old with later, new additions.

The many side altars were elaborate, with tall candles and carved backdrops in gold relief. In the Sanctuary, the High Altar, rich with a shiny tabernacle, polished candlesticks, a carved screen, and a smaller ornate altar in front gave off a blinding light. The altars were dressed in crisp white linen cloths. The High Altar was set off by a red carpet which flowed down the steps to the main body of the church.

A sign told us that,

'The Icod Cross is the best and biggest of silver filigrane (filigree) in the world.
It was donated by a priest who lived in the town.
Height 2045m. Weight 48.300kg.'

Leaving Icod, our guide took us down the mountainside to **Garachico** on the rocky coast below. (I think that due to cancellations we were the only couple on the excursion, but as it was included it had to take place. We therefore enjoyed dedicated one-to-one guidance.) With the hillside above and facing us, we had a splendid view of balconied houses tumbling down the hillside.

On the hillside, you can see the white walls on the side of the road. *(And to think that four years previously we rode up the steep hillside on that little scooter. But it was marvellous, with spectacular views greeting me as I peered down at the rocky coastline spread out far below.)*

In 1706, a tide of lava from an eruption severely damaged what had been the best harbour on this coast. Now, with an opportunity to explore this pretty town further than hitherto, we found ourselves in front of the old port. The *'PILA DE ABAJO.'*

I read the notice which declared that,

'This is all that is left of the old port. There was an eruption a few hundred years ago, which destroyed the port. The remains of the Land Gate are where everyone had to pass under on entering or leaving the port.'

While Allen went into the gardens there to explore, I stayed on flat ground where there were seats placed conveniently to rest awhile. Allen came back through the gardens.

'Oh, you timed that very nicely. He is taking photographs of the old wine press. It is one of the originals.'

I joined Allen in the garden where we had a good view of this huge circular, stone structure; all that was left of the wine press; it was now secured with a fence all around. The selection of plants in the garden was varied; all were flourishing profusely. Going through the town, we came upon yet another church. This one was much simpler than the other one we had just visited, but charming nonetheless, being built in a similar style to the one in Icod.

Many buildings in the narrow, cobbled streets had the traditional Canarian balconies. Down by the harbour, we could see what appeared to have been a loading bay.

My verdict? 'A really interesting little town.' The return visit with a guide and an opportunity to explore further was well worth it.

Santa Cruz de Tenerife.

Santa Cruz de Tenerife is the capital of the island. We had briefly visited here many, many years previously on our first visit to the island and to say the least, had not really been enchanted. On this visit, we reversed our impressions. On reaching Santa Cruz we found that many changes had taken place. Much renovation work was going on along the promenade and main thoroughfare.

We firstly were guided to a jeweller's shop to taste Ron Miel. This is a local drink of Rum and Honey. I drank both mine and Allen's as he did not want to chance its possible effects; I browsed in the display cabinets for my possible birthday present. Did I say that it has been our custom, since we started to come in February for my 50th birthday and have continued ever since, to buy my birthday present whilst abroad? Well, this is a lovely habit and one not to be eschewed albeit a little late this year. Anything worth having is worth waiting for, especially a purchase of lovely ear-rings for my birthday present.

With some free time to wander at will and spying the Little Train (El Tren) which rumbled around the main attractions of the city, we decided to enjoy a ride which took us around the city and into parts, especially the gardens, which we would neither have found, had the time to explore, nor been able to physically walk the distance. El Tren is a feature of most of our holidays and tours. The park in the north of the city was a delightful surprise and so peaceful away from the hustle and bustle of the centre as beautiful fountains played in the sunshine amidst beds of colourful plants.

Leaving the train, we found a shady street to eat our picnic before heading back to the jeweller's shop to purchase the ear-rings which had caught my eye, enchanted to be held up by a crocodile of school children being shepherded across the square. Dressed in a smart school uniform they looked so sweet as they held hands, walking two-by-two as children do the world over.

Re-visiting Candelaria in the North.

The Taganana Valley was one of the more remote parts of Tenerife that we had not visited before. As recounted earlier, this included excursion was the main reason for choosing to stay in Puerto Santiago. That, and the opportunity to see more of the area around Los Gigantes that our previous visits had allowed.

On the way, we stopped briefly at the town of Candelaria which was as windy as experienced on our first visit many years previously. Again, the sea pounded at the sea wall, throwing spray up onto the statues of 'famous people' which lined the side of the square by the sea, in front of the famous church.

I recorded that,

'We are in Candelaria, outside the Basilica of the Black Madonna.'

It lies alongside the sea in an enormous Plaza. Long and low, the walls of the church are white with a contrast of grey stone. The tall bell tower rises high into the sky above the roof of the church. Inside, the octagonal high dome sits above the altar. Behind the High Altar, there are paintings of angels surrounding the Tabernacle in the middle of the altar.

Outside, the roar of the sea in the wind almost drowned out conversation. Undeterred, the lifelike stone statues on tall plinths were unconcerned as they kept watch. Returning to the coach we looked forward with anticipation to the rest of the day into the Taganana Valley.

Taganana Valley.

The excursion to the Taganana Valley was a wonderful experience and, as Mount Teide dominates the island, we could see it from various vantage points as the road twisted and turned on its climb up the mountains. The mountains and valley here are lush and green, in total contrast to the south of the island. The roads snaked up higher and higher to the other side of the mountain and the wild Atlantic coast.

The Taganana Valley is in that most north-eastern corner of Tenerife. Beyond the motorway, lie the very dramatic and verdant Anaga Mountains through which we travelled as we crossed from the Santa Cruz de Tenerife part of the coast to the other 'side' of the peninsula.

Although often misty at a height of three thousand, three hundred and sixty feet (one thousand and twenty-four metres) we were fortunate to be able to see much of the laurel forest as the coach followed the steep, winding, switch-back road. The mist floating above the forest gave off an ethereal feel; we could only look in awe at what nature had created.

The rocks appeared to be like folds of material as they plunged from their great height to the valley below. From the viewing point where we had stopped, it was as if we were on top of the world and could see Santa Cruz spreading out in the distance below the mountains.

'Teide has disappeared again. The clouds are moving so fast.'

This was my last comment before continuing our journey. At one point, we passed caves in the forest; they were still inhabited. From time to time we caught glimpses of the blue sea, a glimpse of the coast of the island of Gran Canaria, goats, and mile after mile of this lush land where white-washed villages were scattered.

At this point, I experienced a lot of 'camera shake' as it was hard to keep a steady hand on the winding mountain road.

Turning to go over the top we found ourselves on the northern side of this tip of the island with the sea on our right side. Again, as in Garachico, along the mountain roadside, white walls had been built to protect you from the sheer drop below. Two brave canoeists braved the swell of the sea.

Arriving in remote Taganana, the sound of the sea crashing on the rocks assaulted our ears. Further out were outcrops of sharp, jagged rocks like small islets around which the surging water of the Atlantic Ocean made its determined way to shore where it paused for breath, leaving a creamy froth in its wake as it returned to the wide ocean. All around, the cliffs rose high to form a spectacular coastline.

In the village, we found a spot where we could eat the packed lunch provided for us by the hotel. After lunch, we strolled along the front, watching in fascination as the surf pounded the rocks. Some hardy souls made their precipitous way down to the harbour from the roadside where the slipway for fishing boats had formed a small beach of black volcanic sand. Two lone surfers braved the elements and pitted their wits against the mighty roar and power of the sea.

A huddle of tightly-packed houses rose above, while palm trees swayed as they bent in the fierce wind. Far below, the sea continued to throw its might against the rock, shooting up a spray of water before quietly sinking back leaving a pool of foam surrounded by a circle of turquoise blue sea against the darkness of the depths.

Los Gigantes from the bay.

Returning from our wonderful experience in the remote far north of the island, we found ourselves back at the bay of Puerto Santiago. Ahead were the dramatic cliffs of Los Gigantes as they swept from their great height to plunge into the sea.

Tucked away behind a rocky outcrop was the harbour that we have chatted about earlier. A yacht in full sail lay in the bay. Now, as I chatted to my husband I recorded for the camcorder.

'A few years ago, we hired a scooter and rode up Mount Teide from the south. We came back from the north coast in the Orotava Valley and again that was a wonderful experience to add to the one today.'

'In the distance, you can see the Clipper Boat which takes people out to see the whales and dolphins. (A boat in full sail was out in the bay.) I was going to go on one of these excursions but when I saw how packed it was I decided not to bother. I am not agile enough.'

Carnival time in Puerto Santiago.

The last of the carnivals took place when we were visiting the island this time. One Sunday we strolled into the centre of town to watch the parade. What a wonderful, colourful sight.

'We are just making our way into Puerto Santiago to the roundabouts where the floats for the carnival will start off their journey into Los Gigantes. I think that this is one of the last of the Carnival activities.'

As we strolled along the road, the sea in the bay was below us with many houses and apartment blocks rising around and above the sea. On the other side of the road, the tall white buildings rose high.

Watching the various floats gather by the roundabout was very entertaining. The first one we saw parked in the street was full of young men dressed in ponchos. The float came complete with a beer barrel the contents of which they lubricated their throats with as they cooled off in the heat and brilliant sunshine. Unfortunately, they had a problem with the engine and we moved on up the street as they tried to make running repairs.

Fiesta time in Puerto Santiago was complete with the sound of steel drums banging out a catchy tune. Fountains on the roundabout splashed cool water. The carnival, which had been due to start at five o'clock in the afternoon, eventually started at six o'clock. The Police who were riding motorbikes got into the spirit of things and thoroughly enjoyed themselves as they exercised crowd and traffic control while joining in the fun. After a long wait the music of bands and floats of vibrant, colourful displays came into view.

The floats were truly magnificent; the costumes on various themes were stunning. The locals of all ages, shapes and sizes from villages around were dressed in colourful costumes in the theme set for their float. Some ladies wore dresses with enormously wide, hooped skirts which swayed along as the wearer jiggled and bounced to the music. Other costumes were scanty but all had the most wonderful headdresses – some of such height that you wondered how the wearer could hold up her head. They must have weighed a ton.

Many of the floats carried children and, of course, there was the Carnival Queen in a lovely white dress sitting on her throne, shaded from the searing hot sun by a canopy above. And the men, bare-chested with close fitting vibrant costumes, danced along in their formations to the beat of the drums pounding out their exhilarating noise. As you can imagine, with the music loud and lively everyone had a wonderful time as the floats made their way to Los Gigantes.

After all the excitement, a cool drink in the shade was the order of the day before we wandered back to the hotel along the sea front for dinner.

Catching our breath, we reflected that we would soon be 'back in business' on the Gold Wing motorbike/trike now that all the refinements were done to the suspension and steering and that we would just 'go for it' and see what was going to happen with the tests and treatment that had been proposed for my husband later that year.

In the meantime, we soaked up the sun as I was very work weary. With a lingering last look at the beach and promenade far below the main road, we put this very different holiday to Tenerife into our expanding box of memories.

******

Our 'island interludes' began with Tenerife all those years ago, and here we are at the end with Gran Canaria being our most recent and last visited island – until, that is, I stick a pin in a map after reading the frequent, enticing brochures which plop on the mat with alarming frequency and say,

'Let's go to . . . ' or 'How about . . . '

And I did.

~ ~ ~ ~ ~ ~

Reflections: A Return to Tenerife

After ten years and many travels later, we are back in Tenerife. Not only because I felt the need for some beneficial winter sunshine, but when I saw the included excursions on offer in the latest winter brochure, I wanted to re-visit some of the areas previously explored.

Citing a 'field trip' to bring our impressions of Tenerife up-to-date. my husband didn't take much persuading once I had convinced him that the terrain in Golf del Sur on the south of the island would be easy enough for walking along the promenade and the harbour/marina near the hotel. I was curious to see what changes had been made to the island in the intervening years.

The day of departure started auspiciously enough with an early start and a taxi to Manchester Airport; we watched the sky lighten as the sun rose. Unfortunately, the heavy clouds on this late February morning obscured any semblance of sunshine and blue skies. We noticed that the cars sitting outside the car parks had a covering of snow. We learned that the temperatures had dropped to minus two degrees Celsius during the night.

Later, after boarding our flight, take-off was delayed. It was going nowhere until it had been de-iced along with all the others that had been there all night. We were number twenty-nine in the queue.

Three and a half hours later our pilot had clearance, once he was finally satisfied that the plane was safe to fly, and we took off for the winter sunshine and warmth of Tenerife south and our beautiful hotel in Golf del Sur on the south coast.

The resort of Golf del Sur.

Golf del Sur appeared to have been largely built for accommodation around the three golf courses in the area. Our hotel was modern, beautiful, and relaxing. It had lovely seating areas and bars, plus a conservatory and patio on the opposite side to the pool area. We could see the marina next door which we found was not as easy to get to, for us, as we expected. We did however manage one stroll for a photo shoot. The rocky coast was accessible but was not flat. We had chosen this hotel above the others in Las Americas and Adeje as we knew that those areas were not flat apart from the promenades.

However, we had many excursions planned and were happy to relax in the hotel in between trips.

Puerto de la Cruz.

With Puerto de la Cruz lying on the north coast of the island, we had been prepared for slightly cooler temperatures than in the south as it was still winter in Tenerife. Leaving the blue skies of Gold del Sur, we headed up the motorway to La Laguna on the eastern tip that juts out at the top point of the triangle. The low cloud was, explained our guide, a dust haze where dust had blown in from the Sahara Dessert in Africa and settled over the island. This haze became thicker and lower as we travelled further towards the north, crossing from south to north at La Laguna. I must say that the infrastructure and condition of the roads is excellent.

Reaching our destination, the few specks of rain did not dampen our spirits but we were thankful for our light jackets. Previously, we had only visited the old town around the harbour. Now, our driver stopped in the more modern part of the town outside a large hotel. Many of the modern high-rise buildings housed hotels, apartments, and shops.

Heading west towards the old town, I was entranced by the number of old but well-maintained buildings with the traditional wooden Canarian balconies seemingly hanging off the wall. One dated back to the year 1730AD.

Modern-day traffic of all kinds – cars, wagons, coaches, motorbikes – vied for space in the narrow streets, at times causing mayhem especially when a van was parked illegally in a bus stop on yellow lines. The policeman who made notes in his pocket book also took a photo on his mobile phone.

Turning inwards down cobbled streets, the hustle and bustle around us was noisy as traders with stalls set up to sell wares of mainly watches and leather goods, invited you to buy. One old building by the harbour housed the Tourist Information Office in one room. A plaque on the entrance wall explains that the Casa de la Aduana:

'. . . was constructed in 1620 and that it consists of the Battery of Santa Barbara, the old defence of the Customs House and the living accommodation of the Prieto-Alfaro family, descendants of the Franchi. The area was known as the true centre of Puerto. Its proximity to La Orotava converted it into a strategic town and in 1648 the town was given the Key of the Island by King Felipe IV.'

Another room had displays of all manner of souvenirs. The most eye-catching for me was the one of handmade lace mats that had drawn-thread work bordering each side.

After a refreshing cup of tea at a coffee shop that also specialised in a range of teas including English Breakfast Tea we wandered back to the coach pick-up point. On the way, we took time to watch the waves crashing into the shore.

Los Cristianos Market, San Juan and Los Gigantes.

A half-day excursion was planned for a visit to Los Cristianos Sunday Market before zooming along the west coast to Los Gigantes and a last stop at the fishing village of San Juan.

An early (first) pick-up gave time to collect guests from the other hotels in the Adeje area before retracing our steps to **Los Cristianos**.

As you will have gathered, we had spent many happy visits to Los Cristianos in earlier years. As it began to be more developed we had moved up the coast to the emerging more select Adeje area which took in the top end of Playa las Americas. The Adeje area, we understood from the Spanish papers at the time, was being developed for the Spanish and a more international mix of clients.

Friends had warned us that in the years since our last visit to Los Cristianos – seventeen years – there had been many changes. They were not wrong.

The land at around the Arona Gran Hotel where we had stayed previously had already started to be developed with improvements to the promenade, apartments, a small parade of shops and a Sunday Market. This area was now very smart; a wide boulevard lined with palm trees ran from the sea front to the main road above. Smart cafés with comfortable seating invited the foot weary to sit awhile. The previous simple market appeared to have been integrated with the shopping mall.

The mountain – *'our mountain'* – that we had trekked over all those years ago was still there – untouched – as it tumbled down to the sea, although more development edged towards it to accommodate sun-seekers. After a cool drink, we made our way back to the coach, a little sad that there had been no time to explore the town again as we had hoped.

The drive north up the west coast took us through and past banana plantations which are prolific in this area, and growing areas of other crops. On our last visit, ten years ago, we had been taken directly to our hotel in **Puerto Santiago** just off the main road. Today, we came down from the mountain road that twisted and turned on its descent to the town giving tantalising glimpses of the giant rocks, that are known as **Los Gigantes**, plunging down to the sea.

With only a one-hour stop, we only had time to wander down the road until we spotted the Harbour Club Café. Here we settled down with a cool drink in the shade of trees and a profusion of plants which tumbled around and waved in the breeze as we gazed out to sea.

At the fishing village of **San Juan**, we had a very short stop by the harbour on the sea front but not enough time to explore further.

Thankfully, back at base, the restaurant was still open for a late lunch after which, replete, we relaxed.

La Laguna, Mercedes Forest and Taganana Valley.

As recounted in the last chapter, we had made brief visits to La Laguna on other tours. Today we were in for a treat as we were due to have a guided walk around the more historical part of the city.

La Laguna, the former capital, is the second largest city in Tenerife and is the University City. Today, the sun shone for us as we drove up from the south coast to the northern tip of the island. As I said at the beginning, Tenerife is triangular shaped with the coast from Las Galletas to Santa Cruz de Tenerife and beyond classed as the south coast.

Passing Guimar (pronounced 'wee mar') we enjoyed clear views of the valley to our left and the old road snaking up the mountain beyond. Arriving in La Laguna, all we had to do was gather in the shady Plaza around the corner from where the coach stopped, whereupon our guide explained that we could either join him or explore.

The tour was essentially following a rectangle around the main historic buildings. Many had the traditional Canarian balconies. One tall building – like a tower – had lattice-work panels at the top, allowing the nuns who lived there to look out but no-one to look in. We were very fortunate in our guide today as, not only was he a native of Tenerife, he lived in La Laguna and knew the city inside out.

The Archbishop's Palace, surrounded on each side by other buildings, had been subject to a devastating fire some years ago. The only way to douse the fire was for a helicopter to hover over the top and drop water bombs to drown the flames and put out the fire. Although gutted inside, we believe that it has been re-built.

Our guided tour ended at the corner where the Cathedral stood. Outside were two large Dragon Trees. Charmingly, a group of school children, all dressed neatly in a colourful uniform of trousers and zip-up jackets, were sitting on the ground as they had their 'outward-bound' lesson.

I found this heartening – that school children were learning about the history and culture of this important city. A group had also been in another building that we had ventured inside to view the traditional Canarian architecture. A central courtyard gave way to rooms for stables and servants while on the upper floor lived the family. These upper rooms had wooden shutters. Our guide pointed out one building which also had a granary above the family room. Servants had to pass through these rooms when needing grain. Hence the family could keep a check on what was being taken out.

At the end of our guided tour of the historic part of La Laguna, we opted to wander back to the Plaza and the café in the Laguna Nivaria hotel that we had been told about. It was a good choice as the café appeared to have been constructed in a courtyard, with easy access to the facilities. A showcase in the bar displayed such a range of gins that I had never heard of. The pot of tea and butter croissant was excellent and not at all expensive.

Leaving La Laguna, we continued crossing the island to the north coast, passing through the pine trees of the **Mercedes Rain forest** and **Taganana Valley** to the small village of Taganana.

Taganana lies on the coast and is reached by a tortuous but stunningly beautiful descent three thousand feet down to the sea, through the Anaga mountains on a winding road with switchback bends. The terraces of cultivated land flowing down the mountainside added to the beauty. With the sun shining in the clear blue sky, the calm waters of the Atlantic lapped at the shore.

We were to have lunch at the Café Africa – named after the old lady who owned it. In Taganana there was one long street housing the few shops and cafés. Café Africa had not changed one iota since our last visit ten years ago. That is part of its charm.

We chose the €9 Euro set meal of wine, water, soup and roll, and plain omelette served with sliced tomatoes. There was a banana for pudding. Bananas as 'afters' appeared to be a regular feature of not only La Gomera which I chatted about earlier.

After a few minutes of enjoying the sea breeze and sunshine, we retraced our steps towards La Laguna but then headed towards the seaside town of San Andres just above Santa Cruz on the south-east coast.

At San Andres, we enjoyed some free time on the sweeping man-made beach where yellow sand had been imported from the Sahara Dessert in Africa. This stop was a pleasant and welcome surprise. The beach was busy with people enjoying the flat beach and waters of the Atlantic Ocean. Our return journey was completed with a swift drive down the motorway in good time for dinner. Another wonderful day and different from the previous visit.

Santa Cruz de Tenerife and Candelaria.

We found that Santa Cruz was largely unchanged. Leaving our coach in the designated area along the sea front, we wandered past the bowl of the huge fountain – now empty for safety during the carnival. The monument that was built to honour those from Tenerife who had given their lives in the Spanish Civil War, stood high and proud, guarded by two larger-than-life warriors. The monument rose high into the sky with a cross carved and mounted into each of the four sides. As befits an important city, many of the buildings were tall and imposing as they slumbered around the Plaza in the winter sunshine. The pedestrian area was pleasant to stroll through and, as usual, we opted for a cool drink at an outdoor café before making our way towards the sea and our coach.

Heading south again, we soon reached the town of **Candelaria**. Turning off the motorway we twisted and turned our way down with tantalizing glimpses of the flower-bedecked streets. Due to parking restrictions – a concert area was being set up in the main square – the coach dropped us off at the entrance to the pedestrianised area.

What a wonderful surprise. Previously, we had simply visited the main square and the Basilica. Now, we had the lively and colourful experience of wandering through the bustle and colour of the many shops and people in the main streets.

Reaching the main Plaza de Patrona as the clock chimed twelve times, we elected to go into the Basilica of Our Lady of Candelaria. We were just in time to take a few photos before Mass began at mid-day. It was cool, quiet and comforting in this beautiful church.

Outside in the sunshine, the bronze statues on plinths of the last nine **Guanche** kings still surveyed the Plaza as they guarded the Atlantic sea which today, gently lapped at the sea wall. This was a total contrast to previous visits when the weather was cold and blustery and the sea spray rose above the sea wall.

Our guide explained that before the Spanish Conquest, Tenerife had been divided into ten kingdoms with a king for each. One king refused to bow to Spanish rule and threw himself off a cliff. The other nine evidently did bow to Spanish conquerors but were subsequently murdered along with all the men while the women were taken alive to be married to the Spanish Conquerors. The bronze statues are of the nine murdered. This was another glorious day.

El Teide and Masca Valley.

Although this was the third time that we had visited El Teide and the second time for the Masca Valley, we were looking forward to a guided excursion where an informative guide would ply us with all manner of information.

After going through the mountain village of **Adeje** (from whence the coastal area took its name), we headed for **Vilaflor**, the last village before **El Teide National Park**. Climbing ever higher, we passed through large areas of pine forest. The day was sunny and clear which was a welcome change after the dust haze of other days. It was so clear that at various points on the journey when we were above the clouds, they appeared to be like a blanket of cotton wool spread in the deep blue sky. It seemed that two mountains rose out of them. In fact, what we were seeing was the island of La Palma in the west which had a dip in the middle. We could also see the small island of **La Gomera** peeping from behind the clouds; it lay between **Tenerife** and **La Palma**.

Before this, we had had a very clear view of the larger island of **Gran Canaria** spread out in the Atlantic Ocean. To allow us to take photos of this beautiful and unexpected scene, our guide organised a stop in a lay-by on the mountain road. He remarked that a van was parked there.

We were greeted by the unusual sight of a tall, thin, man dressed as (we were told) the **Guanches** used to do. With great entrepreneurship, he had set himself up for a photo opportunity which, I should say, many of our party were only too eager to part with €1 Euro for the pleasure; some of them cuddling the baby goat (kid) which he nestled in his arms.

The man dressed as a Guanche wore a hood of what appeared to be goat skin covered with feathers. The hood covered his neck. He was clothed in a short tunic of goat skin and knee-high boots lined with fur/wool. He obligingly demonstrated how he used a big shell for communication by blowing on it and how he could slide down a long pole to descend the mountainside.

By his side was a very modern vehicle for transport; the one parked at the side of the road that we had commented on. He perched on the railings while holding the kid goat in his arms as he gazed out in the sunshine across the far away sea to the island of Gran Canaria in the distance. He certainly knew how to pick his spot for earning some money.

Climbing higher, we left the pine forests to enter **El Teide National Park**. Here, the volcanic rock formations told their own tale of the development of Tenerife since it erupted from the sea bed many millions of years ago. Each layer or seam of a different colour represents a different eruption. I had not realised before today that there were other mountains around Et Teide. Our informative guide soon dispelled that erroneous assumption.

The contrast of pine trees growing among the different colours of lava rock was startling. In addition, other low, smaller plants grew in abundance. Our guide explained that as plants need soil and can't grow in rock alone, the dust and sand – the Calima – blowing in from the Sahara Desert in Africa eventually provided the means for growth.

After a coffee stop at the Mirador, the cable car station café, we headed down on a different road unaware of the entrancing treat awaiting us.

Turning off the main road to the **Roques de Garcia**, the most astounding rock formations left from an eruption took our breath away. Essentially, these rock formations were in a crater, the sides of which had eroded away in places to leave the unique and fantastically shaped towering rock formations of a glowing, deep, rust colour.

After everyone had taken all the photos they wanted to – after negotiating the steps gouged out of the crater – we made our way down the mountain again. Our guide pointed out the lava lake. Black lava could be clearly seen where it had flowed down the mountain from an eruption.

Above all this astounding beauty, El Teide stood proud and high – the highest mountain in Spain. Although we had had a flavour of the area on our previous two adventures, it proved that an official guided excursion is the best option.

Nearing lunch-time, we stopped at the charming coastal village of Chio where the owners of El Rancho were waiting for us with a simple lunch of soup or Spanish omelette, bread, wine or water, and coffee or tea. Chio is near the village of Guiá de Isora and was on our way to the Masca Valley. The restaurant was bedecked in heavily flowering bougainvillea on the terrace. Potted plants abounded while others contrasted with the white walls and the rustic feel presented to the onlooker.

Moving on, we headed towards the **Masca Valley** and the towering Teno Massif which dominates every twist and turn of the switchback road that first climbed high before flowing down into the valley. We were now in the north of the island. La Palma was still visible against the clear blue sky as it nestled on its bed of cotton wool-like clouds.

At Masca, which hangs off the mountainside with only about one hundred inhabitants, we had a photo stop outside the town square. The wind was fierce to say the least as we negotiated the short path down to the Plaza. A small church sheltered in the rock at one side while an old tree dominated the centre, its branches casting a welcome shade. There was the usual shop and bar for souvenirs with the addition of the use of facilities for a small payment. At the top of the road, other cafes and bars met the needs of tourists.

The journey back along the same switchback roads was an entertainment as vehicles coming the other way nervously crept past the coach, or even more nervously backed up to allow the coach driver to negotiate the bends which were bordered with huge blocks of stone to stop an unscheduled descent down the mountainside. Scooters of course, simply zoomed through the narrow gaps between the cars and coaches.

The coach drivers on all our excursions deserved a medal, as did the guides for their fund of knowledge. Our guide today was a native of Tenerife but spoke excellent English which he told us was compulsory in the schools to learn along with – at secondary level – another optional language making three in all which was essential for tourism. To learn to speak English properly he came to England and studied in the city of Bath. We also noticed that road signs such as 'BUS' and 'STOP' are in the international language of English.

After yet another glorious day, we arrived back at our hotel in good time for our last dinner before packing in the morning for our return home.

(We did enjoy one other excursion on this latest visit to the island. Our ferry ride to La Gomera which I chatted about earlier.)

******

And now we come to the end of our Atlantic adventure and our meanderings in the Mediterranean – for now. Who knows what the future holds for us?

What we do know is that having grasped every opportunity to push back our boundaries and explore, we are thankful that we have done what we can while we can.

In truth, we cannot say 'if only'.

Bibliography

http://www.gomeralive.com/ferry-fred-olsen/

Map of Mediterranean.
Mediterranee_02_EN.edited.photos.jpg.
By-O.H.237 – own work, CC by SA,4.0.
https://commons.wikimedia.org/W/Index.php?curid=
38364150. http://commons.wikimedia.org

Map of North Atlantic.
Courtesy anniebissett.com
http://www.nationalgeographicexpeditions.com/exped
itions/island-odyssey-azores-canaries/detail

Map of Sao Miguel.
New-Sao_Miguel_Physical_map-wikimedia.orgedited.jpg
http://commons.wikimedia.com

Map of Canary Islands.
1280px-Map_of_the_Canary_Islands.svg-
wikimedia.jpg. Google images courtesy Wikimedia.org.

Postcard map of Gran Canaria by Andrés Murillo
S.L.

More about Rosalie Marsh's Books

Just Us Two Series.

During their first Gold Wing motorbike experience, finding that the words flowed when recounting their profound emotional experiences, Rosalie Marsh realized that there were the beginnings of a story. Eventually, their adventures developed into a travel series of which *Island Interludes* is the latest adventure *when Just Us Two Escape to the Sun* from the hectic pace and demands of life.

All travel books and the travel-based fiction are in hardback, paperback, and eBook formats for most devices. *Just Us Two* travel books contain photographs.

Just Us Two: Ned and Rosie's Gold Wing Discovery. Second Edition 2012.
ISBN 978-1-908302-12-0 Perfect Bound Soft Cover.
ISBN 978 1 908302-24-3. eBook.
ISBN 978-1-908302-49-6. Hardback.
Winner 2010 International Book Awards. Finalist 2009 Best Book Awards (Travel: Recreational category).

Ned and Rosie found their lost youth when, in middle age Rosie discovered a Honda Gold Wing motorbike. They set off to realize Rosie's dreams of finding her roots in Ireland before exploring Europe.

Chasing Rainbows: with Just Us Two.
ISBN 978 1 908302-00-7. Perfect Bound Soft Cover.
ISBN 978-1-908302-25-0. eBook.
ISBN 978-1-908302 50-2. Hardback.

Chasing Rainbows is the real ending to Rosie's Gold
Wing motorbiking story as they mentally say good-bye
to their beloved Gold Wing motorbike but until after
more adventures.

The Long Leg of Italy: Explore with Just Us Two.
ISBN 978-1-908302-39-7 Perfect Bound Soft Cover.
ISBN 978-1-908302-44-1. eBook.
ISBN 989-1-908302-51-9. Hardback.

A journey of discovery and adventure as Rosie explores
Italy from the lakes and mountains in the north, the
elegant cities of Rome, Florence, Venice, and Sorrento
and down to the very tip of the toe of Italy

**Island Interludes: Just Us Two Escape to the
Sun.**
ISBN 978-1-908302-43-4. Perfect Bound Soft Cover.
ISBN 978-1-908302-45-8. eBook.
ISBN 978-1-908302 52-6. Hardback.

As their travel horizons widened and they continued to
push back their boundaries Rosie and her husband took
every opportunity to 'experience the culture, sights, and
sounds of islands previously only dreamt of as they
escaped to the sun.

***

Fiction

ORANGES: A Journey.
ISBN 978-1-908302-31-1 Perfect Bound Soft Cover.
ISBN 978-1-908302-46-5 eBook.
ISBN 978-1-908302 48-9. Hardback

Marsh's debut fiction is a contemporary fantasy built on a dream. Introducing Charlotte to the world, this mixture of fact and fiction takes the reader into Portugal and Spain. But are they dreams? Or reality?

***

Lifelong Learning: Personal Effectiveness Guides.

The series draws on Marsh's extensive skills & industrial experience in sales management and work-based learning in adult and further education. Initially, the series looks at the background to lifelong learning and some research into various viewpoints. The series continues with four user-friendly 'workshops in a package'.

Whom are these books for?
- Aimed at the Home Learner and designed to read in bite-sized chunks.
- Someone who is unable to attend formal courses.
- To fill gaps in underpinning knowledge and skills needed to 'get on in life'.
- Designed as a user-friendly support material for learners of all ages with a wide range of abilities.

All books are in paperback and eBook formats for most devices. All books in the series are illustrated.

Lifelong Learning: A View from the Coal Face
ISBN 978-1-908302-04-5 Perfect Bound Soft Cover.
ISBN 978-1-908302-26-7 eBook.

This springboard for the series is based on a research paper that looks at learning, opportunity, access, professional and personal development and asks if the initiatives in this area worked. The research is brought up-to-date with some post-research reflections in the light of the *Wolf Report*.

Release Your Potential: Making Sense of Personal and Professional Development.
ISBN 978-1-908302-08-3 Perfect Bound Soft Cover.
ISBN 978-1-908302-27-4 eBook.

After looking at the process of professional and personal development, Marsh follows with an introduction on how to structure and develop your continuing personal development records.

Skills for Employability Part One:
Pre-Employment.
ISBN 978-1-908302-16-8 Perfect Bound Soft Cover.
ISBN 978-1-908302-28-1 eBook.

Marsh looks at those skills for the future, which include preparing for work, Job applications, and successful interview, working effectively in the workplace and basic ICT skills in the workplace, legislation, and progression.

Skills for Employability Part Two:
Moving into Employment.
ISBN 978-1-908302-20-5 Perfect Bound Soft Cover.
ISBN 978-1-90830229-8 eBook.

Marsh looks at the standards of behaviour and requirements of employers. These include Employment Rights and responsibilities, the business environment, working relationships, customer service, managing your money and healthy living before looking at progression.

Talking the Talk: Getting the Message Across.
ISBN 978-1-908302-35-9 Perfect Bound Soft Cover.
ISBN 978-1-908302-30-4 eBook.

Are you often in a situation where you have to give a talk, presentation or staff briefing? This book will help you to prepare well, become confident and overcome nerves, and deliver an interesting presentation that will be remembered for the right reasons.

What people say.

"A highly effective trainer, coach, and assessor who strives for excellence in everything she does. Her knowledge of work-based learning and adult education is outstanding and she offers good support to those she teaches and mentors, particularly through drawing on her own personal experience as an adult learner."
Andrew Ellams, MD Ellams Associates Ltd.

"An inspirational individual and dedicated professional who gives and shares only her best. She's been very thoughtful and creative in her visionary approach to support the education sector, strengthen stakeholder relationships and guiding individuals to achieve their aspirations and goals."
Prabhjit Kaur – PGCE(FE,) CMgr MCMI, Assoc.CIPD, MBA(Open).

"A detailed and passionate professional, who loves to share her knowledge."
Joanna Kinch, MD Ebenezer Properties Ltd.

Rosalie Marsh titles are available worldwide in print and e-book formats for most devices.

[i] The Long Leg of Italy: Explore with Just Us Two
[ii] The Long Leg of Italy: Explore with Just Us Two

Christal Publishing

Lightning Source UK Ltd.
Milton Keynes UK
UKOW01f0651050917
308612UK00014B/700/P